A crew that time forgot

RUBISLAW TO RUHLEBEN

Margie Mellis
and
Doreen Black

Published in October, 2018

Copyright © Margie Mellis and Doreen Black

The right of Margie Mellis and Doreen Black to be identified as author of this book has been asserted.

A catalogue record for this book is available from the British Library.

ISBN 978-0-9570999–9–9

Design and typesetting by Leopard Press
LePress@btconnect.com

Printed and bound in Scotland by
Robertsons, Forfar

Published by Leopard Press
Auld Logie, Pitcaple, Inverurie, Aberdeenshire AB51 5EE

Contents

Acknowledgements

Thanks are due to the following:

The **Royal Horticultural Society Lindley Library** staff for all their help. **Fiona Davison,** Head of Libraries and Exhibitions for her encouragement and permission to use information and photographs from their Ruhleben Archive. Special thanks are due to **Cai Parry-Jones,** Digitisation manager, and **Crestina Forcina** for their patience and help and to **Liz Taylor** from the archives department.

John Edwards and the staff at Aberdeen's Maritime Museum for their help and advice.

Aberdeen University's Special Collections for permission to reproduce the photos of the *S.S. Rubislaw.*

Gary Thomas, Archive Assistant at Aberdeen Journals for permission to reproduce the article on Captain Walker's return and the image of Alexander Garden's card, and the *Daily Express* for permission to reproduce the photo of Captain Nicolson.

Elizabeth Blunt for her support and for providing archive material owned by her mother, Margaret, David Tulloch's daughter.

Charles Wilson's granddaughters **Pearl, Gert, Doris** and **Nan** for sharing their memories of their grandfather.

Janice Davidson for her key role in setting up the project.

Janice Gill and **Kate Blackburn Roffey** for information about their relatives George Wyllie and James Blackburn.

Our husbands **Jim** and **Robert** and our families for their endless patience, support and interest.

And, of course, our editor **Lindy Cheyne** and designer **Ian Hamilton** for all their support and advice.

How it All Began

MARGIE MELLIS writes:

Some years ago now, my mother's cousin, Nan Robertson, showed me a cutting from the *Scots Magazine*. The writer of the letter was trying to find out more about his grandfather, George Barron, who had been a prisoner during World War I in a civilian camp in Germany called Ruhleben. He had been on board a ship called the *Rubislaw*.

Knowing I was interested in family history Nan told me that her grandfather, my great-grandfather, Charles Wilson, had also been on board the *Rubis-law*, and he too had been interned.

I had never heard the story before; indeed at that time I had never heard of Ruhleben, and I asked her if she had replied to the letter. She said she had not because she could tell him nothing. My attitude was that he might have been able to give her some information about the whole affair. I did write to the author of the letter, but it was already some years old by then and I did not get a reply. So first of all I went back to family sources.

Charles Wilson had five sons and one daughter.

Charles Wilson, with Gert and Pearl

His wife, Tina McLeod, died in 1920, during an operation to fix a badly set broken ankle, and, as often happened when a wife died, the only daughter, Annie, took over the running of the household. Her two daughters, Nan and Doris, both born in the 1920s, were therefore brought up with their grandfather, and remember him well, and probably heard more stories than my mother did. Their cousin, my mother, daughter of one of his sons, visited frequently, and was very much in awe of him. I have photos of her and her sister standing beside him looking on their best behaviour.

Following up family stories is one of the interesting things about researching your family history, and I determined to find out more. Photographs of the *Rubislaw* in Aberdeen Harbour Board's George Washington Wilson collection gave me contemporary images of the ship, and at Aberdeen's Maritime Museum I saw a builder's half-model of the *Rubislaw*, and got her specifications. This gave me the official number of the ship which enabled me to write to the Maritime History Archive at the University of New-

The *S.S. Rubislaw* in Aberdeen Harbour

foundland for the crew list or manifest at the time of the *Rubislaw*'s trip to Germany in July 1914.

A query in the *Aberdeen & North-East Scotland Family History Society Journal* brought a helpful reply from a fellow-member, who alerted me to the existence of the Prisoner of War records in Aberdeen City Archives. Articles that had appeared in the local press at the time furnished me with a wealth of contemporary information, about the *Rubislaw* herself, and about the experiences of her crew and of some of her passengers.

A great deal has also been written about Ruhleben internment camp itself, in newspaper and journal articles of the time in both this country and in Germany, and in books and academic articles written after the war.

Then more recently, I read an article in the *BBC News Magazine* about a horticultural society set up by the prisoners in Ruhleben, which was to be the focus of an exhibition set up by the Royal Horticultural Society (RHS). One of their sources was a Doreen Black whose grandfather, David McKay

Tulloch, had been in the Ruhleben society. I recognised the name of her grandfather as one of the crew of the *Rubislaw*.

Through the Society I was able to get in touch with Doreen, and we are now in regular contact. This contact resulted in an invitation to the opening of the exhibition in London where we were able to meet. Since then the two of us have been trying to put together a story about the camp, the ship, and the crew of the *Rubislaw* whose routine voyage ended in a way nobody expected.

There is a further family connection with the *S.S. Rubislaw*. She was built in Aberdeen by Hall Russell & Co., shipbuilders, founded in 1864. My other maternal great-grandfather, William McGruther, was a boilermaker in Hall Russell's and worked on the *Rubislaw*. His son-in-law, my grandfather, who was Charles Wilson's son, became an apprentice there and was also in the shipyard in 1904 when the *Rubislaw* was finished.

When I mentioned to a retired Hall Russell employee that my grandfather had been a boiler-

Hall Russell workers

maker with Hall Russell, he replied, "Oh, one of the kings," and went on to say that the boilermakers were the most skilled and highly regarded of the work force.

Aberdeen Harbour

The S.S. Rubislaw

In 1904 Aberdeen shipbuilders Hall, Russell & Co. launched a steel-screw cargo steamer. It was built for the Granite City Steamship Company, specifically for the trade between Aberdeen and Hamburg. The ship was named the *Rubislaw*.

A large number of guests were invited to the launch on 24 November and they gathered afterwards in the company's headquarters for a cake and wine reception to wish success to the ship and to her owners. As well as a large cargo-carrying capacity, the *Rubislaw* had first-class passenger accommodation, a point which was made much of in the speeches at the launch. It was suggested, to much laughter, that the Harbour Commissioners might find this very useful.

Later on, more seriously, the chairman of Hall Russell's pointed out that Aberdeen Harbour badly needed shear legs so that bigger ships could be built, and that the Harbour Commissioners might perhaps avail themselves of a trip to Hamburg to see what there was there as regards shipbuilding facilities.

In the month after the launch, the *Rubislaw* had

the distinction of being the first vessel to pass through the opening of the new Regent Bridge. This bridge and the adjacent works were the first instalment of the scheme for the modernisation of the harbour at a cost of £120,000.

In his speech at the opening ceremony of the new Regent Bridge, Shoremaster Milne said: "It is most appropriate that the first vessel to signal for the new bridge and demand a passage should be the fine screw steamer, *Rubislaw*.

Built by a local firm of shipbuilders, owned by one of the Harbour commissioners, named after a district of our good city Bon Accord, and proceeding on her maiden voyage, we will hope that these three characteristics augur well for the future usefulness of the bridge."

The *Rubislaw* was delivered to the owners in January 1905, and her trial trip in Aberdeen Bay took place on Thursday, 12 January 1905, after which she immediately set sail for Bo'ness to take on bunker coal before proceeding to Hamburg for the first of many successful voyages.

The 1914 voyage

On Friday, 31 July 1914, the *Rubislaw* left Aberdeen on her usual voyage to Hamburg. The trade between the two cities had grown so much by 1914 that the *Rubislaw* made the round trip every 10 days. On this particular trip she carried 18 of a crew and nine passengers.

The voyage was uneventful and they arrived in Hamburg on Sunday, 2 August. The cargo was discharged as usual. The passengers disembarked and went their separate ways, some intending to spend only a couple of days in Hamburg before rejoining

the ship for its return voyage. On Tuesday, 4 August, Great Britain declared war on Germany. Early on the Wednesday morning, the Hamburg authorities informed Thomas Walker, the *Rubislaw*'s captain, that he would be allowed to depart, and by the time the ship was ready to sail later that day, about 130 British citizens had crowded on board, anxious to leave Germany for home. Steam was up and the pilot and tug in readiness when they were told they would not be allowed to leave that afternoon after all.

Britain's declaration of war had come as a surprise to most Germans as well as to the British. Britain and Germany had a shared cultural heritage, there was a long history of trade relations between the two countries, the royal families were closely connected. They were our 'cousins'. So it is perhaps not remarkable to learn that some 7,000 British subjects found themselves in Germany when war was declared in August 1914: a large number of people living and working in Germany, students at German universities, golf and football professionals, music students, hundreds of visitors who were on walking holidays, attending the many music festivals, or "taking the cure" at the German spas. And of course there were the officers and crew of merchant vessels, over 1,200 of whom were in German ports.

The German government was totally unprepared for these hordes of "enemy aliens" and at first they were allowed to go about their business as usual, on condition that they reported regularly to the police.

However, one group was less fortunate – the merchant seamen. The crew of the *Rubislaw* were informed that they would not be allowed to leave the ship, and the vessel was taken to the middle of the harbour and moored there. And there they remained for two months and 10 days while the German authorities decided what to do with them.

Meanwhile at home, relatives waited anxiously for news. This was before the days of instant communication, and it was not until some three weeks after the declaration of war, on 21 August, that the *Aberdeen Daily Journal* was able to report, "*Rubislaw* passengers and crew safe". A letter had been received from the American Consulate General in Copenhagen, informing the owners of the *Rubislaw* that the crew and passengers were safe in Hamburg. The United States Government, as representatives of a neutral country, had taken responsibility for the protection of British subjects in Germany and Austria-Hungary.

However, Charles Wilson's wife, Tina, had received some reassurance before official word came through. Charles's sister, Elizabeth Milne, and her daughter, Jessie, who lived in Dundee, were interested in spiritualism, like many people at the time. Shortly after war was declared they visited a medium, who saw a man sitting in a dark place with his head in his hands. He wanted his family to know that he was safe and well.

On 15 October the merchant seamen, the crew of the *Rubislaw* among them, were moved to abandoned, rotting, rat-infested hulks in Hamburg harbour. Captain Walker, the captain of the *Rubislaw*, gave a graphic description of the conditions there: "The crew... were bundled into hulks like a lot of sheep, without bed or bedding, or covering of any description... The food was shocking. All they got was a piece of black bread in the morning, with black coffee without sugar or milk, and the dinner was composed of a soup made from rotten maize and putrid pigs' feet." This was in marked contrast to the British merchant seamen in the nearby port of Bremen. They were taken from their ships and housed decently in hotels.

The official German attitude was that Germany had no quarrel with civilians and that they would eventually be shipped home, but a campaign in the German press demanded retaliation for the internment of German civilians in Britain. By mid-September 1914 there were 13,500 internees held in Britain, mainly from the large German civilian community. The German authorities issued an ultimatum to Britain, stating that unless all German civilians were released by 5 November, every British citizen in Germany would be interned.

As John Ketchum put it in his book, *Ruhleben: A Prison Camp Society*: "The ultimatum was ignored, the orders went forth, and on November 6 every male British subject between the ages of 17 and 55 was placed under arrest. In police vans, by taxi, and on foot, the Engländer were collected and lodged in the nearest jails; from these they were transferred in batches to the place assigned to them – a deserted race-track on the western outskirts of Berlin. There, in the stables once tenanted by race-horses, most of them were kept for the next four years."

This was Ruhleben, where the 18 men of the *Rubislaw*'s crew arrived in November 1914.

The Crew of the Rubislaw

Who were these 18 men who made up the crew of the *Rubislaw*? Well, they were all Aberdonians. Their ages ranged from 17 to 60.

Most of them had sailed together before – the only exceptions were Charles Wilson, the steward, and James Baird, an able-seaman and carpenter. Both of them had signed on for that particular voyage to replace crew members who had been discharged.

Thomas Walker, the captain, was 60 years old. He had been captain of the *Rubislaw* since 1905, replacing the original captain, George Milne, shortly after the launch of the vessel. He knew Hamburg well, and spoke German fluently.

After the captain, the oldest member of the crew was Charles Wilson at 55 years of age. He was an experienced ship's steward and had sailed regularly on the North boats to Orkney and Shetland.

Under him he had an assistant steward, Alexander Mackie, who was 30, and a cook, George Barron, who was 36.

In addition to catering for the crew, they had to

	SIGNATURES OF CREW	Age	Nationality (if British, state birthplace)	Year	Ship in which he last served, and Year of discharge therefrom. State Name and Official No. or Port she belonged to.	Date	Place	In what capacity engaged	No. of certificate	Amount of Wages per Week	Amount of Wages Advanced upon or at the time of Engagement	Amount of Weekly or Monthly Allotment	Signature or Initials of Official or other before whom Engaged	Date	Place	Cause	Release of Wages paid on Discharge	We, the undersigned...	Signature or Initials of Official or other before whom Discharged		
1	Wm. Walker	60	Aberdeen	1914	"Rubislaw" Aberdeen	7/7/14	Aberdeen	Master	16220				JW					(Released 18/10/15)			
2	J. W. Pattison	31	London	"	do	do	do	Mate	039160		2 4 4		JW				*				
3	James Greig	52	Aberdeen	"	do	"	do	Boatswain			1 16 9		JW					(Released 24/12/15)			
4	Wm. Bruce	34	do	"	do	"	do	Lamps AB			1 17 4		JW				*	(Released to Holland 23/2/18)			
5	Alexander Steele	22	do	"	do	"	do	AB			1 15 -		JW	27.7.14	Aberdeen	Discharged	1 15 0	Alex Steele	J.W.P.		
6	Thomas Hughes	36	do	"	do	"	do	AB			1 15 -		JW				*	(Released to Holland 23/2/18)			
7	Francis Johnston	53	do	"	do	"	do	AB			1 15 -		JW					(Released 24/12/15)			
8	Fred Bryce	1st	do	"	do		do	OS			1 1 -		JW				*				
9	James Shepherd	1st	do	"	do		do	OS			1 1 -		JW				*				
10	D. M. Tulloch	58	Forres	"	do	"	do	1st Engineer	36		3 5 4		JW				*				
11	Alex Rennon	29	Aberdeen	"	do	"	do	2nd do			1 19 1		JW				*				
12	Angus Leith	49	do	"	do	"	do	Fireman			1 17 4		JW					(Released 9/1/18)			
13	Jas. Graham	29	do	"	do	"	do	do			1 15 -		JW				*				
14	Alex Inglis	36	do	"	do	"	do	do			1 15 -		JW					(Released 6/10/16)			
15	W. J. Forbes	33	do	"	do	"	do	do	1785		1 15 -		JW					(Released to Holland 23/2/18)			
16	A. Campbell	48	do	"	do	"	do	Steward			1 15 -		JW				*				
17	A. Mackie	30	do	"	do	"	do	assistant steward			- 14 -		JW				**				
18	G. Barron	36	do	"	do	"	do	Cook			1 10 4		JW				*				
19	J. Baird	31	do	"	do	29.7.14	do	AB			1 15 0		J.W.P.				*				
20		53																			

prepare the meals for the passengers who sailed on the *Rubislaw*. The steward was in charge of the overall operation, but a very important part of his job was to assist the captain in entertaining the passengers and in contributing to the conversation at table, while the cook had to provide the lavish meals of the time to satisfy the passengers.

The cook, George Barron, had been on the *Rubislaw* for some years. In 1910 he and George Erskine, the steward at the time, had pleaded guilty to smuggling 65 pounds of tobacco and a quantity of Geneva spirits and rum on board the *Rubislaw* from Hamburg.

The two men said that they were intended as Christmas presents, but they were both fined, George Barron more heavily since this was his third offence. It was obviously not something the company regarded as a reason for dismissal, though.

The chief engineer on the *Rubislaw* was David McKay Tulloch (38), Doreen Black's grandfather. He lived in Osborne Place in Aberdeen with his wife and three children. Like Captain Walker, he knew Hamburg well.

Doreen has a small notebook belonging to her grandfather in which there are lists of items with prices and whether or not paid. According to his granddaughter he had made many friends in Germany over the years he had been on the Aberdeen/Hamburg run, and it appears that these lists were items he had been commissioned to buy for his contacts in Germany. He also took goods back with him for friends in Aberdeen. Doreen remembers two beautiful china dolls he brought back for his daughters.

Germany was well-known for its bisque or porcelain dolls. The lists of goods he bought in Germany include other children's toys such as wooden monkeys on a stick, performing clowns and jumping dogs, and items such as leather goods, scent, cigars, Kropp razors and amber and ivory beads.

The first mate of the *Rubislaw*, Thomas How Pattison, was 31. He had been born in London, but his mother, Mrs Chatterji, was living in Aberdeen. Her husband was a merchant in India, and she was reasonably well-off.

Doreen Black remembers her grandmother being in contact with other wives whose men were in Ruhleben, and I have a photograph of my grandmother (Charles Wilson's daughter-in-law) taken some time after the war, in the early 1930s, with a Mrs Chatterji who must surely be Thomas Pattison's mother.

James Shepherd and Fred Bryce, young lads of 17, were both ordinary seamen, effectively apprentices who were on board to gain experience at sea in order to become able seamen. The mothers of both men were widows, and Fred Bryce's mother died in December 1915.

Besides Charles Wilson, there was one other newcomer to the crew, James Baird. He was 28, an able seaman and carpenter, whose father was manager of the Nether Don Salmon Fishing at the old Bridge of Don. Before signing on, he too had been a salmon fisher.

When these 18 men sailed into Hamburg on Sunday, 2 August, they expected to be back in Aberdeen within the week, but it would be some time before they saw their families again.

The crew ages given in brackets are taken from the crew list for the voyage at the end of July 1914. Unless otherwise stated, the men were in Ruhleben until the end of the war.

CAPTAIN:

Thomas Walker (60) had been master of the *Rubislaw* since 1905, shortly after her launch. He lived with his wife, Euphemia, at 51 Abergeldie Road. Captain Walker's health suffered as a result of his internment, and he spent the last six months of his captivity in the sanatorium at Charlottenburg in Berlin, before being repatriated in October 1915.

FIRST MATE:

Thomas How Pattison (31) was the Chief Officer or First Mate and received a weekly wage of £2 4s 4d. He lived with his mother, Mrs

Chatterji, at 8 Devanah Terrace. He was interned in Barrack 4 at Ruhleben.

SECOND MATE OR BOATSWAIN:

James Cumming (52) was the boatswain aboard the *Rubislaw*. He received a weekly pay of £1 16s 9d. He was released on the grounds of age in December 1915.

ABLE SEAMEN:

An Able Seaman has several year's experience at sea. The Rubislaw's able seamen earned £1 15s per week.

James Baird (31) was a carpenter. His father was the manager of the Nether Don Salmon Fishing, and James was himself a salmon fisher. Like Charles Wilson, he was not a regular crew member, but signed on for this particular trip. He was in Box 27 of Barrack 9 in Ruhleben.

William Bruce (34) was an able seaman and lamptrimmer. This was a specialist position on a steam vessel where oil lamps were important for navigation and visibility, and this responsibility was reflected in his pay of £1 17s 4d, which was slightly more than that of the other able seamen. He was married with three children, and lived at 240 King Street. In Ruhleben he was housed in the loft box of Barrack 3. He was released in March 1918.

Thomas Hughes (36) was married with a child, and lived at 35a Union Street. He was in Box 27 of Barrack 9 in Ruhleben, as was James Baird. He was released in March 1918.

Francis Johnston (53) was released in December 1915 on the grounds of age.

ORDINARY SEAMEN:

An Ordinary Seaman has little or no experience at sea and needs 'sea-time' before he can become an Able Seaman. The Rubislaw's ordinary seamen, both young men of 17, received £1 1s per week.

Fred Bryce (17) lived with his mother at 17 Roslin Street. She died in December 1915. Bryce was in Barrack 22 at Ruhleben, but later moved to Barrack 5.

James Shepherd (17) lived with his mother and four siblings at 93 Park Street. The family later moved to 38 Watson Street. Like Fred Bryce, Shepherd started in Barrack 22 and then changed to Barrack 5.

1ST ENGINEER

David McKay Tulloch (38) was Chief Engineer on board the *Rubislaw*, earning £3 5s 4d a week, the highest paid crew member after the Captain. He was married with three children, and lived at 66 Osborne Place. He was in Barrack 9, Box 19 at Ruhleben.

2ND ENGINEER

Robert Whitton Cameron (29) was the Second Engineer, earning £1 19s 1d per week. He was married and lived at 88 Menzies Road. He was in Barrack 11, Box 26 at Ruhleben. Like many of his fellow-crew members in 1914, he rejoined the *Rubislaw* when she resumed sailing to Hamburg in 1922. By 1939 he was the Chief Engineer. In September of that year the *Rubislaw* struck a mine and sank. Robert Cameron was one of 13 crew members who went down with the ship.

FIREMEN

James Graham (29) was married and lived in 97 West North Street.

William George Forbes (33) was married with five dependants, and lived at 82 East North Street. He was in Barrack 9, Box 27 at Ruhleben. He was released in March 1918.

Alexander Inglis (36) was married with seven of a family, and lived at 3 St Clements Place. He was in Barrack 9, Box 27 and was released in August 1916 on the grounds of ill health.

Angus Mackie Leith (49) was the donkeyman, responsible for the small donkey engine or auxiliary engine used for pumping water into the boilers. His pay reflected this extra responsibility, and he received £1 17s 4d where his fellow firemen received £1 15s. He was married with six children, and lived at 11 South Mile End. He was released in January 1918.

The Galley

Charles Wilson (55) was the steward on board the *Rubislaw*. He signed on at the last moment in place of an A. Campbell. His pay was £1 15s per week. He was married with five adult children, and lived at 10 Summerfield Place. He was released early, in December 1915, along with James Cumming and Francis Johnston, on the grounds of age.

Alexander Mackie (30) was the assistant steward or mess room boy, earning 14s per week. He lived at 15 Kintore Place.

George Barron (36) was the cook, earning £1 10s 4d. He was married and lived at 25 Justice Street. In Ruhleben he was in Barrack 8, in the north end of the loft.

CONTACT THE AUTHORS

The authors would be pleased to hear from anyone with connections to or information on the crew and passengers of the *S.S. Rubislaw,* or other Aberdeen men who were in Ruhleben camp.

rubislaw1914@gmail.com

Aberdeen Harbour: In the early 20th century all travel to the continent was still by sea.

The Passengers

The *Rubislaw* was not just a cargo vessel; she also had excellent passenger accommodation. As well as the crew, the *Rubislaw* was carrying nine passengers when she set out for Hamburg on 31 July 1914. In the early years of the 20th century all travel to the continent was still by sea, and in those days before mass foreign tourism cargo ships usually carried passengers as well.

Although international travel was becoming more popular, passports were not required, on the whole, for travel within Europe, and crossing a border was a relatively straightforward procedure. Consequently, comparatively few people held passports. During World War I, however, the rules were tightened for security reasons, and these controls remained in place after the war, a move which was very unpopular with British tourists who especially resented having to supply a photograph and a physical description.

The sea trip to Europe was part of the holiday: a report in the *Aberdeen Journal* of Monday, 23 September 1907 states that throughout that particular season the *Rubislaw* had had a full complement of passengers for every voyage, and "all are loud in praise of her qualities as a sea-going boat, and of the attention they receive from the steward... who heartily assists the captain in making matters pleasant for the passengers".

Another article in the *Aberdeen Journal* of Saturday, 5 August 1905 gives a much fuller account of a typical voyage on the *Rubislaw*. This report, Aberdeen to the Elbe by the *S.S. Rubislaw*, was written by a press reporter, and his description of the voyage makes it clear that it was an enjoyable and interesting one, and, as he states, "at a cost within the reach of those with even comparatively limited means." Once again the steward is mentioned – he "kept a splendid table," and the meals were "capitally served".

The ship had left Aberdeen on the Tuesday evening, and after dinner the passengers went on deck to enjoy the summer evening before going below for a rubber of whist and an impromptu concert. On the Wednesday morning they arrived in Sunderland, where the passengers were able to spend the day ashore while the cargo was unloaded. There was time for an excursion to nearby Roker with its brass bands and Pierrot shows. In the evening the *Rubislaw* set sail for the passage across the North Sea. Thursday was spent relaxing in deck chairs, enjoying the sun. After another convivial evening the passengers were up early on Friday for their first sight of Heligoland, and were able to watch the sights and the activity as they entered the mouth of the Elbe and sailed the 70 miles upriver to the port of Hamburg.

On this particular trip, the *Rubislaw* was in port for five days, and the captain, Thomas Walker, who knew the city and the language well, spent those five days acting as a guide to the *Aberdeen Journal* reporter, showing him the busy harbour and the city of Hamburg itself, "the greatest port in the world".

The return journey was as pleasant as the outward voyage. At midnight the *Rubislaw* passed through a great fleet of trawlers, the lights of which resembled a large village, and this was seen as one of the highlights of the voyage. The reporter concludes that he can confidently recommend the Granite City Steamshipping Company's vessels for any Aberdonian who wishes to spend a holiday on the continent with the maximum of comfort and the minimum of cost.

The nine passengers who left Aberdeen on board the *Rubislaw* on 31 July 1914 would have enjoyed a similar passage, at least on the outward journey. The captain was still Thomas Walker. The ship arrived in Hamburg on the Sunday and the passengers disembarked, and went their separate ways. The passengers mentioned in the press as being safe and well are therefore presumably those who had booked for the return passage from Hamburg to Aberdeen. These included several who had intended to stay only the few days the ship was in port before returning with the *Rubislaw*. Some of the passengers have been identified, and it is interesting to note their reasons for being in Germany; some were on business, some for study, some were there purely for pleasure.

On 20 August 1914, Messrs Richard Connon, Reid & Co., managers of the *Rubislaw*, received a letter signed by five of the passengers and sent from the American Consulate General in Copenhagen, informing them that the passengers and crew of the *Rubislaw* were safe. The passengers are named as: James Craik of the Northern Agricultural Company, John Milne of the Aberdeen Commercial Company, Mr True, senior master of languages at Robert Gordon's Technical College, who, as was his usual custom, was spending a holiday in Germany, Mr A.D. Garden, a student at Aberdeen University, and James J. Paterson, a doctor, accompanying Mr Garden. British civilians who found themselves in Germany at the outbreak of war were initially allowed to go about their business as usual, on condition that they reported regularly to the police, and many found accommodation locally in hotels or with German families.

One of the passengers, referred to only as a "gentleman", managed to get back to Aberdeen on another ship, and reported on 28 August 1914 that the passengers still in Germany were very comfortable. Four of the men had got good accommodation in the house of a professional gentleman in Hamburg, and the Misses Mackay, Aberdeen teachers, had also got comfortable accommodation and were very pleased at the way they were being treated.

The gentleman in the report may well have been Mr Emil Theodor True of Robert Gordons Technical College, whose resignation is reported in the *Aberdeen Journal* of 23 September 1914. According to the article, the order declaring Aberdeen to be a prohibited area for enemy aliens, "has had an immediate effect upon several well-known Germans, who have occupied professional positions in Aberdeen for many years". This was certainly the case with Mr True who had been in Scotland for over 30 years and who lived with his unmarried sister, Adela, in Gray Street.

Mr True is reported in October 1914 as being part of a "small German colony" in Banchory. Aberdeen was a prohibited area, and many German nationals in Aberdeen had been moved to Banchory, which, being in Kincardineshire, was therefore in an unprohibited area. At this stage, the men were not interned, but had to stay within five miles of their residence.

Gustav Hein, who taught German at the Girls High School in Aberdeen, was also in Banchory, awaiting news of his application for naturalisation. He too had lived in Aberdeen for over 30 years, was married to an English woman, and their children had all been born in Aberdeen.

Alexander Garden, a young man of 20, was a medical student studying at Aberdeen University. Germany was known for its research-based approach to medicine and a knowledge of German would have been important for a student interested in the latest medical developments. Like all British subjects who found themselves in Germany in August 1914, he was allowed to go about his business as usual provided he reported regularly to the police. It wasn't until the beginning of November that British civilians were arrested and sent to Ruhleben.

His friend, Dr James Paterson, was the medical officer for Maidenhead. He had left Aberdeen for Hamburg on 31 July, intending to spend only a couple of days ashore before returning. But he too was arrested and told not to leave Hamburg. He eventually managed to get a passport from the American Consulate and tried to get home by way of Holland. He was stopped at the frontier and sent to a concentration camp in Hanover, but was allowed out when doctors were told that they would be permitted to leave. When he returned home he was able to report that Alexander Garden, John Milne and James Craik were still in Hamburg. In fact, he returned home on 6 November, the very day the men were rounded up and taken to Ruhleben.

John Milne, of 17 Sunnyside Road, Aberdeen, was in Germany representing the Aberdeen Commercial Company, shipowners. He was the son of the late Captain George Crombie Milne who had commanded the *Linn o' Dee* and was the first skipper of the *Rubislaw*. His friend, James Craik, lived at 7 Mile-End Avenue with his mother, a widow. He was a book-keeper at the Northern Agricultural Company, manufacturers of artificial manure, whose premises were at Blaikie's Quay in Aberdeen. The two men tried to obtain passports, and having failed, stayed in a hotel for a week, and then moved into private lodgings with a German family, where they stayed for almost three months before being removed, first of all to the lodging hulks in Hamburg harbour, and then to Ruhleben.

Finally, the Misses McKay, sisters Nellie and Mary, both primary teachers, had gone to Germany on holiday with two of their friends. When Germany declared war on Russia on 1 August, they were in Königsberg in the east of Germany, and were advised by the American consul there to return home immediately. They eventually managed to reach Hamburg where they were able to secure a passage on the *Rubislaw*. When the *Rubislaw* was unable to leave they found accommodation locally, and, after having secured passports from the American consulate, they reached home by way of Rotterdam and Flushing.

On her return in September the younger Miss McKay, Nellie, gave a graphic description to the *Aberdeen Journal* on the attitude of the German people to the British. She talked about the "war fever" they experienced in Berlin, but said that there was no sign of this in Hamburg. In Hamburg, with its cosmopolitan population and trade associations with Britain, there was little sign of anti-English feeling.

Women were permitted to leave Germany, as were doctors, boys under 17, and men past military age. Younger men who were of an age to enlist were not allowed to leave the country, and were eventually sent to Ruhleben.

Among the men sent to Ruhleben were *Rubislaw* crew members Charles Wilson and David Tulloch. These two men had very different experiences of Ruhleben.

Charles Wilson

Ruhleben 1914 – 15

After three weeks confined to the detention hulk moored in Hamburg harbour, the crew of the *Rubislaw* were moved to Ruhleben. David Tulloch writes in his notebook: "On 6 November 1914 taken from detention ships and sent to Camp at Ruhleben Spandau."

On that same day, all British male civilians between the ages of 17 and 55 were also rounded up and transferred from all over Germany to Ruhleben. Some 4,000 men, all non-combatants, were confined together in this camp on the outskirts of Berlin.

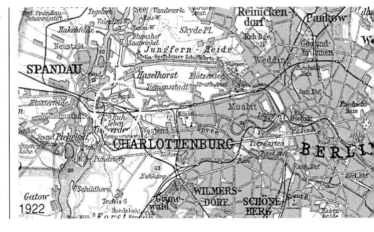

Ruhleben 1914-15

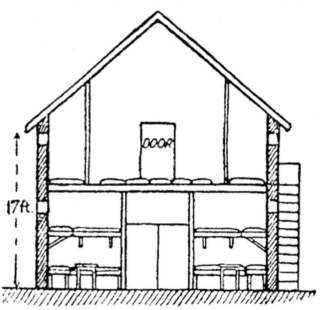

SECTION THROUGH BUILDING

Reproduced by permission from the " Daily Mail."

Transverse section of a Ruhleben barrack. The upper half shows the loft containing about a hundred beds; the lower half shows two horse-boxes containing six beds each arranged in two tiers.

What met them as they arrived at this place that was to be their home for the next four years? Ruhleben was the name of the harness or trotting racing track which had been in use right up to the start of the war. The site covered 10 acres and had a racetrack and stables for the horses with lofts above the stables for the straw. Little preparation had been done by the Germans to house all these prisoners; in fact they were overwhelmed by the number of men, about three times as many as they had expected.

There were 11 buildings for the horses. These buildings were referred to as 'barracks' by the German authorities. The horses had been removed but their dung and the straw still remained, and one of the first things the prisoners had to do was to clean out the horse boxes. Each box had contained one horse, but six men were expected to share this small space. There were six iron beds in tiers of three and a table in each box, and each man was given some straw for the bed and a horse blanket.

However, the men in the horse boxes were at

least better off than the men who ended up in the haylofts, where in some cases there wasn't even room to sit up straight, and where, if they turned over in bed, they disturbed their neighbours on either side. One hundred men were crammed into each of these lofts, sleeping on straw on the bare floor. Nine more barracks were built in the following year, but until then there simply was not enough room to house all the men, and conditions were very cramped and overcrowded.

David Tulloch was housed in Box 19 of Barrack 9, the same barrack, although not the same box, as several other members of the *Rubislaw*'s crew – Robert Cameron, Thomas Pattison, and the Captain of the *Rubislaw*, Thomas Walker, were all in Barrack 9, and Thomas Hughes, Alexander Inglis, William Forbes and James Baird all shared Box 27 in the same barrack. In fact, this barrack was dominated by seafarers, as to a lesser extent, were Barrack 8 and Barrack 4, and they were all generally referred to as 'sailors' barracks'.

This was November, the horse boxes had floors and walls of concrete, and there was no heating. The nights in particular were bitterly cold. The inside walls and the ceilings were frequently covered with ice, and the men's breath congealed. They slept in their outer clothes and still weren't warm enough.

There was no ventilation, and only a dim light in the corridor, and many of the men found that their eyesight suffered as a result of trying to read or write in these conditions.

Sanitary arrangements were completely inadequate. The men had to queue to wash in cold water which came from one tap, and the latrines which had been dug for the prisoners were described later by the American ambassador as "a danger not only to the camp but to Berlin". It was not until February 1915, three months after the camp was first occupied, that a boiler house was built and hot water became available. It was built by the prisoners themselves with funds from the American Embassy.

The months between November 1914 and February 1915 were very cold with bitter winds coming

The undersigned Aberdonians, now civil prisoners of war in Ruhleben, Germany, wish the Lord Provost, Magistrates, Town Council, and Citizens of Aberdeen a Happy and Prosperous New Year.

Robert L. Brown   John S. Milne
Robert W. Cameron   John S. Milne
James Craig   W Noble
Robert Forbes   Thomas H. Paterson
A.D. Garden   Allan Ritchie
L.J. Harold M.B.   David M. Tulloch
Alf Hill B.Sc.
Alexander C. Milne   Thomas Warren
George A. Wyllie

Abt David M. Tulloch
Barrack 9   24th December 1914

The above is a reproduction of the interesting postcard received on New Year's Day by Lord Provost Taggart. All the signatories are well-known natives of Aberdeen and district who are meantime interned in an English prisoners' camp "somewhere" in Germany.

from Poland and Russia, and there was a great deal of rain which quickly turned the sandy soil of Ruhleben into a quagmire. Men found themselves ankle-deep in mud wherever they walked. Through this mud the men had to walk about a quarter of a mile three times a day to queue for their food from the camp kitchen.

Conditions might have been more tolerable if the men had received adequate food. But food was in very short supply, and what there was, was almost inedible. The prisoners had to rely on parcels sent from home, and things improved once the official parcels service was set up. The importance of these food parcels to the prisoners cannot be overestimated. As the war progressed in fact the prisoners in Ruhleben had far better food than the general population of Germany.

That first Christmas of 1914, the Lord Provost of Aberdeen, James Taggart, received a postcard with

◀ How the *Evening Express* reported news of Aberdeen's civil PoWs on 5 January 1915.

the signatures of 16 Aberdonians who were in Barrack 9 in Ruhleben. The men wished him, the Magistrates, Town Council and citizens of Aberdeen a happy and prosperous New Year. Several crew members of the *Rubislaw* signed the card as did three of the *Rubislaw*'s passengers, James Craik, John Milne and Alexander Garden. The men had drawn straws to find out who should actually send the card, and David Tulloch was chosen. Some weeks later, the men received a reply from the Lord Provost, expressing the wish that they would get home soon. On his card, Taggart included a short poem:

> *To all concerned*
> *Who are interned*
> *Far from the Silver City*
> *We send to you*
> *Our sons so true*
> *Our warmest love and pity*

When the German authorities had hurriedly set up the camp, the Prussian aristocrat Gerd Graf von Schwerin-Sophienhof had been appointed as its

Commandant. He was a former chamberlain to the Emperor. Count Schwerin was a kindly elderly gentleman, sympathetic to the men's predicament, and very conscious of his responsibilties towards them.

He felt strongly that his duty was to protect them, not to bully them. His deputy, Baron von Taube, was responsible for the day-to-day running of the camp. Like Schwerin he was not unsympathetic, but tended to lose his temper and he worried about what his superiors in Berlin might think. Some of the guards on the other hand were sometimes overofficious and brutal in their treatment of the prisoners. These guards were usually disciplined and removed from duty.

One particular incident early on in the life of the camp earned Count Schwerin the men's respect. Orders had come from Berlin that no smoking was to be allowed in the camp. Schwerin got in touch with the War Office in Berlin, pointed out that smoking was one of the few comforts available to the men, and said that unless this order was rescinded, both he and von Taube would resign. The order was rescinded, but he warned the prisoners that the authorities in Berlin could easily cut off the supplies of tobacco and that the men should try and get hold of us much as they could themselves.

The prisoners were not a homogenous group. Among those taken into custody were businessmen, professional sportsmen, musicians, academics and students, and of course many tourists. But by far the largest single group of men, over 1,000 of them, about a third of the total population of the camp, were the merchant seamen. As well as being a large occupational group, the seamen differed from the other prisoners in the range of their ages. All other male civilians between the ages of 17 and 55 had been interned, but the seamen were swept up indiscriminately, and there were about 50 or 60 boys, some as young as 15, interned in Ruhleben, and some men as old as 75.

In general, these seafaring men coped better with the conditions in the camp, accustomed as they were to life on board ship with its cramped conditions, and to periods of absence from home and their loved ones. In his book, *Ruhleben: A Prison Camp Society*, John Ketchum feels that Ruhleben would have been a different camp without its seafarers, "softer, less virile, top-heavy with intellectuals". He goes on to say that, "it was their courage that set the first high standards, and their healthy Philistinism that kept the later cultural life in balance. They were tough in language and manner. Their patriotism was unwavering. Above all, the seafarers were a stabilizing influence in a restless and mercurial population. Grumblers by profession, they damned the conditions of the camp in the foulest terms, but at the same time bore them more philosophically than the landsmen. Not easily enthused about anything, they were equally hard to depress; their common sense, steadiness, and ironic humour were of incalculable value to Ruhleben".

As a civilian prisoner of war camp, Ruhleben was very much in the international public eye. At the outbreak of the war, the United States, at that point a neutral country, had assumed responsibility for British interests in Germany, and the U.S. embassy in Berlin took this role very seriously. Only a matter of months after the transfer of prisoners to Ruhleben, the American ambassador to Germany, James W. Gerard, visited Ruhleben for the first time and was appalled at the poor sanitation and the overcrowded conditions in the camp. As a result of his complaints, improvements began to be made, and some men were released, but only those who were unfit for military service.

When Charles Wilson was released on grounds of age and arrived back in Aberdeen in December 1915, he mentioned to the Aberdeen Journals reporter a "curious incident" that had occurred at the camp. It had obviously made an impression on him. A military commander had come round and had asked all who were in sympathy with the Germans to stand out. Out of the 5,000 men in the camp, Charles Wilson said, about 700 lined up, probably, he thought, because they expected to be released.

This was an incident involving a large group of prisoners in the camp who in the eyes of the other prisoners were German, but who in the eyes of the German authorities were English. The question of German nationality was complicated, and a child of German parents who was born in Britain or a

British colony was regarded as British even if that child had subsequently lived in Germany from an infant, and spoke no English. And it took several generations before an immigrant to Germany was regarded as German. These men, English in the eyes of Germany, had been rounded up with the other Englishmen. And then there were men whose work had taken them to Germany and who had been there for many years. They had married German women, their children had been born in Germany. Some men had lived in Germany all their lives, and German was their first language. But unless they had been born in Germany to German parents, they didn't have German nationality. Much the same situation prevailed in Britain where men who had lived most of their lives in Britain, and who regarded Britain as home, were shocked to realise that they had suddenly become enemy aliens.

And of course many of the men who were rounded up were in Germany enjoying German culture, German music, German scenery. Many will have known some German. Captain Walker, for example, could speak German fluently, and David Tulloch understood and spoke some German.

There was a certain amount of friction between these men who regarded themselves as German or who were settled in Germany, and the British prisoners. Matters came to a head when Baron von Taube received a complaint about a remark made by a British sailor, in which he referred to "bloody Germans". Von Taube assumed 'bloody' was the same as the word 'blutig' which suggests 'drenched in blood'. British propaganda had painted the Germans as barbarians killing Belgian babies, so this was a sensitive subject. A special roll call was called, and von Taube harangued the prisoners and commanded those who considered themselves to be good Germans to stand forward. Many did, and some obviously believed it, feeling that they should never have been interned in the first place, and that it was a mistake which would eventually be rectified. Others probably felt that this might be their chance to be freed.

One of the prisoners had been Professor of Eng-

Among those taken into custody were businessmen, professional sportsmen, musicians, academics and students, and of course many tourists.

lish at Berlin University and he and some of his fellow linguists later took von Taube aside and explained the meaning of the word 'bloody' to him, and its fairly frequent colloquial use, especially among the seafarers.

The incident made matters worse and accentuated the differences between the two groups who up until then had managed to live reasonably well together. The authorities in Berlin heard what had happened and, as a result, the pro-Germans were segregated from the other prisoners, and a list of reasons for a German prisoner to be freed was drawn up. A distinction was also made between those who considered themselves German and wished to give up any association with Britain, and those who, despite the war, still felt respect for Germany, its ideas and culture, but who had no wish to give up British citizenship. If this had been clarified in the beginning, it would have saved a lot of trouble.

Shortly after the men arrived at Ruhleben, von Taube ordered each barrack to appoint a captain. These captains had to be fluent in both German and English and were to be the intermediaries between the prisoners and the military authorities. The captains formed a committee and Joseph Powell was appointed as overall camp captain. Once that had been established, order within the camp was maintained by the prisoners themselves. Little obstruction was put in their way, and it was obviously in the German interest to have the camp administered properly.

One of the first things the committee did was to compile a list of things which needed to be addressed. On the list was the question of the seamen's luggage. Over 1,000 seamen had arrived in Ruhleben wearing only the clothes they stood up in. They had not been allowed to take anything with them when they were taken from their ships. In his notebook David Tulloch has a list of what he had to leave behind. In addition to his books and mathematical instruments and his bed linen, there was his uniform, his working clothes and 'go ashore' clothes, including a straw hat, a soft hat and a bowler hat. A hat for every occasion. This of course was at a time

Left on board SS "Rubislaw"

1 Suit goashore clothes £3-15
1 " uniform " 2-10
2 pairs working trousers 1-12
2 Jackets & two vests
1 Umbrella
2 Caps (uniform)
1 Straw hat
1 Soft hat
1 Bowler hat

3 Boiler Suits
4 working Shirts
2 goashore "
3 pairs under pants
2 flannel undervests
2 pairs boots 1 pair Slippers
1 pair Slippers (leather)
2 pair gloves
4 towels
1 Scarf
12 collars & collar box
12 ties assorted
9 pairs Socks
2 T Squares
3 Set Squares
1 Set of Scales
1 Case drawing tools
1 3' Rule (Steel)
2 12" Straight edges
1 Square
1 Bag of tools assorted
1 Belst brace (Small)

1 Brest-brace (Large)
1 Electric Lan
2 feather Pillows
2 Blanket
2 Sheets
1 Bed cover
1 Matress
1 Set Modern Engineering 9/-
1 Clock
1 Reids Engineering book
1 Dozen Glasses
1 Set of Studs
1 pair cuff links
1 overcoat
1 pair Spectacles
1 Set brushes & case
6 Linen hankerchiefs
2 cusions & covers
1 Settee cover
6 Pictures & frames
1 Indicator (McInnes)
1 Life line
4 pairs Out Callipers
2 inside Callipers
1 " Jenny willows
1 6 Bt edge
1 3 "

when a man would not leave home without wearing a hat.

The committee were extremely efficient. They appointed vice-captains, organised funds to purchase neccessities such as cleaning materials, and to pay the men who offered to do the cleaning; they appointed postmen, cashiers, firemen, laundrymen; they organised a police force.

On 15 September 1915, three months before Charles Wilson was released, Count Schwerin sent for Joseph Powell and told him that there had been too many problems with the German guards, and that the prisoners seemed to cause less trouble when left to themselves. He proposed that the guards should be withdrawn from the actual camp, and that the various camp captains should take full responsibility for the prisoners.

So towards the end of 1915, Ruhleben and its prisoners started to develop into a self-governing community. According to the camp captain Joseph Powell, who wrote a history of Ruhleben in 1919, his book was written "to show how a number of Eng-lishmen, raked in from the German cities, dumped in a swamp, and housed in stables, set to work to found a British colony and build a British city within a few miles of the enemy's capital".

In December 1915, after 17 months of captivity, Charles Wilson was released from Ruhleben on grounds of age. After his return to Aberdeen, he never spoke about his time as a prisoner of war. He was an older man, 55 when he was interned, an old-fashioned husband and father who was used to life at home revolving around him. What probably made matters worse was that he was not a regular crew member on the *Rubislaw*, and it was pure chance or bad luck that he was on the ship in the first place. It meant also that he didn't really know his fellow crew members. A few months before he was repatriated conditions in the camp did begin to improve slightly, but he had experienced the worst of Ruhleben, the appalling conditions, the sometimes brutal treatment by some of the guards, the inadequate food, the lack of purposeful activity, the boredom. His experiences in Ruhleben were negative ones.

Help from Home

Meanwhile, what was happening at home? When war was declared in August 1914 people at home naturally wanted to help in any way they could, and there was an immediate drive to provide tobacco, warm clothing and other comforts for the troops. In Aberdeen and the surrounding area, the 'troops' were the Gordon Highlanders. Women and schoolgirls knitted socks, gloves and scarves, while individuals collected other items which might be needed to support the soldiers at the Front.

In Aberdeen, one woman, Mary Niven, realised that in the midst of all this patriotic fervour, one group was being entirely overlooked – the prisoners of war and others held in German camps. In most cases they had no clothes other than the ones they stood up in, and they had no facilities for writing home. She decided to do something for these prisoners, and in December 1914 she placed an advert in the *Aberdeen Journal*, asking for warm clothing, socks, shirts, tobacco, pencils and postcards, as well as financial contributions.

Mary Stewart Niven was the wife of Charles

Mrs Mary Niven, 1894, by Charles William Mitchell

Niven, Professor of Natural Philosophy at Aberdeen University. She knew Germany well, and in fact had been there when war was declared. Thanks to her knowledge of the language and her awareness of German red tape, she had managed to get home without any difficulty, but she knew that not everyone would find it as easy to cope with the system.

From her home in the Chanonry, she and her two daughters, Mary and Lucy, with the help of two assistants, spent their time preparing parcels. Send-

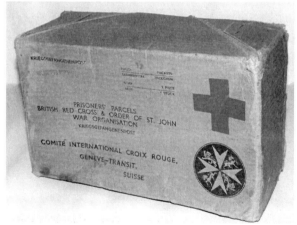

ing parcels to the camps in Germany was a completely different proposition from sending comforts to the troops at the Front where everything was conveyed through Army channels. Mary Niven realised that the main problem was addressing the parcels properly to ensure that they arrived safely, so she made sure they were carefully wrapped with the inner and outer wrapping addressed in both German and English. In addition, she enclosed a return-addressed postcard for the men to send back,

so that she would know the parcels had arrived. Money was never sent. This was time-consuming work, and Mrs Niven asked for volunteers to help, in particular young ladies with a knowledge of German.

This operation was on a very large scale and in November of 1915 Mary Niven made an appeal in the press for subscriptions to send a Christmas Box to over 1,000 prisoners. These were men who belonged to Aberdeen or were in the Gordon Highlanders. They were each to receive a parcel containing a plum pudding, a currant loaf, one pound of cheese, six mealie puddings, half a pound of tea, sugar and salt.

The families of the *Rubislaw*'s crew had been doing whatever they could from the start. As soon as they knew where their menfolk were, they began sending individual parcels to them. They knew from reports in the press about the appalling conditions in Ruhleben, and about the shortage of food and its poor quality, and realised that sending food was very important. At the beginning of 1915,

Jan 7th 1915

Jan 14th 1915 recieved parcel from home, including 1 Shirt, 1 pair socks, 1 pair mitts, 1 Cake, 1 piece cheese, 1 Box chocolate, 1 Box biscuits.

Jan 15th: Told us we were B. English

Thursday Jan 21st, 1915. Potato Soup for dinner with an over dose of acetic acid in it. Rotten

Friday 22nd Turnip Soup made with pigs feet. (Very Salty)

Saturday 23rd Cabbage Soup Rotten

Sunday 24th. Pease & Carrots. 8.7

Monday 25th. Rice potatoes + meat 7

Tuesday 26th Cabbage Soup no potatoes no meat (Rotten)

Wednesday 27th. K. Birthday Potato Soup + meat 8.7

David Tulloch records in his notebook that the men were living on "potato soup for dinner with an overdose of acetic acid in it – rotten" or "turnip soup made with pigs feet – very salty" or "cabbage soup – rotten". When the parcels started arriving from home, he carefully wrote down the details: parcels contained items such as "tea, cocoa and milk" or "hat, collars and tie and loaf of bread" or "bread, cheese, pineapple and one tin biscuits and darning wool". These lists frequently have "Thank God" in brackets after them.

In the early stages of the war, these were largely individual efforts, but as the war progressed it became more organised and other bodies took over. Mary Niven's initiative had become increasingly important, and by late 1915 had grown to become the Aberdeen Prisoners of War Bureau with offices in the Albert Hall in Huntly Street. Its work was to send out parcels of food and comforts to soldiers, sailors and civilians belonging to the northeast of Scotland who were prisoners in German camps. Relatives of these men were asked to notify the Bureau.

On 14 December the County Clerk of Aberdeen wrote to the Chief Constable with a request from "some of the ladies" connected with the Bureau for a complete list of all the prisoners of war, whether military, naval or civil, belonging to Aberdeen City and the counties of Aberdeen, Kincardine and Banff, "so that they may make as sure as possible that every prisoner belonging to that area is receiving assistance in food and clothing".

The names and details of 12 crew members out of the *Rubislaw*'s crew of 18 are to be found in the Aberdeen & District Prisoners of War Bureau Men's Ledger, now in Aberdeen City Archives, and they throw some light on the circumstances of the men themselves and of their families at home.

Five men had been released before the scheme was properly set up. Of those remaining the chief engineer, David Tulloch, is mentioned as being in Barrack 9, Box 19. His wife was living in Osborne Place, but the ledger notes that while the house was the property of the prisoner, "it is heavily bonded". She received £1 per week through the Shipping Office, but this was all she had to support herself and three children. Her husband had been earning over £3 per week.

The Bureau agreed to send a weekly food parcel, to supplement those she was already sending. In his notebook, Tulloch mentions a parcel from the Aberdeen Prisoners of War Bureau for the first time on 11 April 1916. It contained oatcakes, mealy puddings, salmon, milk, quarter pound of tea, two pounds sugar, half pound bacon, margarine, syrup. By the beginning of December of that year, Tulloch, like several other members of the crew, started receiving parcels from the Merchant Seamen's Help Society, a national organisation whose secretary was Mrs Neeld, instead of from the Bureau.

Seventeen-year old James Shepherd was also sent weekly food parcels by the Bureau, and later from the Merchant Seamen's Help Society. His mother was a widow, receiving 10 shillings from the owners of the ship, and nine shillings per week from the Parish to support herself and four dependents. This still amounted to less than her son's weekly wage of one pound, one shilling. Despite the fact that she had so little herself, she had been managing to send regular parcels. Many other women at home were struggling to cope with reduced incomes, but they were still sending regular parcels to their husbands, sons and brothers in Ruhleben.

Other members of the crew had less need of help. James Baird's father was manager of the Nether Don Salmon Fishing at the old Bridge of Don, and he was "in good circumstances" and able to "send all that the prisoner requires". The Bureau notes that Mrs Chatterji, mother of the mate, Thomas Pattison, had a husband who was a merchant in India, that "she declines to give particulars of income" and that she was sending a parcel of food weekly and paying for bread to be sent from Switzerland.

This bread from Switzerland was sent to prisoners in Germany by the Red Cross whose main parcel collection and distribution was centred in Berne, in neutral Switzerland. The Red Cross aimed to provide each prisoner with one 10lb parcel and 13lbs of bread every fortnight. It was perhaps the largest and best-known organisation to provide food to prisoners during World War I, but many other welfare and charitable associations, voluntary groups and individuals throughout Britain played a vitally important part in sending parcels.

There is no doubt that the efforts of all these organisations, and of friends and family, were crucial to the well-being of the prisoners, not just in terms of physical health, but also in helping to lift their spirits. In his preface to Geoffrey Pyke's book, *To Ruhleben – and Back* (1916) Paul Collins points out that "visiting diplomats and Red Cross officials were so appalled by the thousands of starving and sickly men, that by 1916 Germany was embarrassed into improving conditions slightly".

When he was released on the grounds of ill health in October 1915, Captain Thomas Walker, master of the *Rubislaw*, said: "If it was not for the parcels received from home, the prisoners would be starving", and Charles Wilson agreed that "the food we got was not sufficient to keep a man alive, but

Aberdeen and District Prisoners of War Bureau,

County Buildings, Castle Street, Aberdeen, Scotland.

22ᵈ *March* 1916.

This Committee has sent to you by post to-day, a parcel of food and comforts, with its good wishes. In the parcel is a list of contents. An acknowledgment to the Committee, or to it through any of your relations, will oblige. If you are in need of any special article, please report. If you know of any person in your camp belonging to this District who is not receiving parcels, kindly send the Committee his home and internment addresses.

after we were three months there the parcels began to arrive from home, and but for that we would have been starved."

▲ The Aberdeen P.O.W. Bureau agreed to send David Tulloch a weekly food parcel, to supplement those that his wife was already sending.

Ruhleben 1916-18

In the summer of 1916, only six months after Charles Wilson arrived back in Aberdeen, Count Schwerin, the Commandant of the camp, was showing a distinguished American visitor round a Ruhleben which Charles Wilson would scarcely have recognised. The visitor complimented him on the state of the camp, and on the variety of activities which had been provided for the men.

"You mustn't suppose," Schwerin replied, "that the camp was always like this. When the men were first brought here, the place wasn't fit to keep pigs in. All that you have admired in the camp they have themselves created."

What had changed in such a short time? What had the men created? What did the visitor see and admire? What confronted him was a bustling community, a community with purpose.

Conditions had improved. New barracks had been built, and this, together with the release of some of the older men, meant that there was much more space in the camp. The German authorities had provided cinders and ashes from the nearby rail-

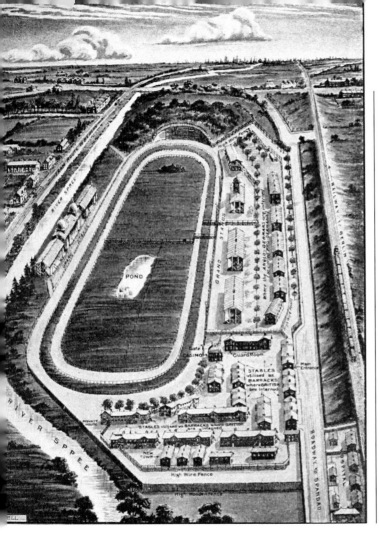

way to spread on the paths in the camp, and railway sleepers to put down as walkways when the weather was bad.

The food was improving too, and becoming more plentiful. Food parcels were arriving more regularly. Parcels from friends and relatives at home were supplemented with parcels sent by official organisations. David Tulloch notes that the first parcel sent by the Aberdeen Prisoners of War Bureau arrived on 11 April 1916 and every week after that. The German administration seems to have been very efficient in ensuring that the parcels reached the camp. The parcels were opened in the presence of the prisoner, partly to make sure there was nothing forbidden in them, and partly to ensure that everything was there that should have been. Things did sometimes go missing though. David Tulloch's wife had been sending regular parcels of food and clothing to her husband, but a pair of boots she sent had never arrived. So she hit upon the idea of sending the boots separately. And this time he did get them. When he finally arrived home in Aberdeen, his wife, his two daughters and his son were waiting to greet him on the station platform. Seven-year-old Douglas could scarcely have remembered his father, but he did recognise the boots.

Round about the same time as the official parcels started arriving, permission was given for a private cookhouse, and this meant that the men could now heat the contents of the tins they received. In general the men were better fed than the majority of the German civilians, especially as the war progressed. Britain was successfully blockading the German ports and preventing food from getting through.

The American ambassador, James Gerard, continued to keep a close eye on the welfare of the prisoners and made recommendations and negotiated on their behalf. The British government was very generous in the allowance of money for prisoners in Ruhleben and was happy to provide whatever was needed.

The Race Track Association in Germany still owned part of the track at Ruhleben, and Gerard was able to hire this from them. This meant that more sports could be played, and it also provided more ground for the flourishing Ruhleben Horticultural Society. They had been keen to grow more vegetables, but had not had enough space. There is no doubt that the number and variety of vegetables grown by the prisoners greatly improved the men's diet in the last couple of years of the war. David Tulloch was a member of the RuhHS, and it was here that he learned the techniques of gardening.

From the very beginning of their internment, the prisoners had started to organise diversions, activities designed to keep boredom at bay and give some structure and meaning to their lives. As civilian prisoners of war they could not be forced to work. This was an advantage of course, but it did mean that their time had to be filled in somehow. There was a daily roll call, waiting in queues to wash, and to fetch their food, but in between there was nothing to do. So the men had to find their own ways of passing the time.

Card games and board games were played from the beginning, as was football. At first this was just

'Roll Call' on the field at Ruhleben in September 1917.

kicking a ball around, but there were many professional footballers in Ruhleben, and before long a Ruhleben Football Association was formed and a league was set up.

A Debating Society was set up, and a Sports Committee. So many well-known and talented musicians, some with their own instruments, had been in Germany in August 1914, that it was not long before a choir was set up and an orchestra, and regular performances were given. There was a

Dramatic Society which produced performances of a very high standard.

As camp life developed and more and more people became involved in the activities, the men settled down and began to look on Ruhleben as home. In the first months of the war, discussions between Britain and Germany about the exchange of prisoners had meant that there was always the thought of home and possible repatriation, and the camp was regarded as merely temporary. But talks between the two countries broke down and gradually most of the men began to accept the realities of the camp and embrace its opportunities. A real community began to develop. Class differences in Britain in the early 20th century were very marked and there was a clearly defined social hierarchy. It is perhaps not surprising that this was mirrored in Ruhleben, and that despite the men's common circumstances, social distinctions asserted themselves almost from the beginning. Some of the men who had been at public schools set up their own private club in a hut, and paid some of the poorer prisoners to act as servants, for example.

And there was also a hierarchy among the seamen. Others in Ruhleben might not be aware of it, but there was a big difference between the fishermen and the merchant seamen, and within the merchant seamen there was the distinction between officers and crew. The ships' captains were a group apart, and Molony paints a nice picture in his book, *Prisoners and Captives*, of seeing three or four little red lights about five feet, four inches from the ground moving backwards and forwards in a line. These lights were from the pipes of the sea captains pacing an imaginary deck and never uttering a word.

Because the men in Ruhleben came from all walks of life, they were able to offer a wide variety of services to their fellow-prisoners. Small businesses were set up where you could get your hair cut, or your shoes mended, or engraving done. Skilled carpenters made souvenirs of Ruhleben, artists painted portraits or supplied views of the various parts of the camp.

In a letter to his wife dated 15 November 1917,

David McTulloch

Baracke 9

Box 19

Nov 15th 1917

An —To M Mrs Tulloch   Ort Aberdeen

Osborne Place   -Straße No. 66

GELD IST AN INTERNIERTE **PERSÖNLICH** ZU SENDEN / MONEY TO BE SENT BY POSTAL ORDER
UND ZWAR AUSSCHLIESSLICH DURCH POSTANWEISUNG. / ONLY, NOT PER REGISTERED LETTER. —
— AUF DER RÜCKSEITE DES ABSCHNITTES IST DER / ADDRESSEE'S FULL NAME MUST BE WRIT-
VOLLE NAME DES EMPFÄNGERS ZU WIEDERHOLEN. / TEN LEGIBLY ON COUNTERFOIL SLIP.

My Dear wife - Just a few more lines to say that I am still keeping well, trusting this will find you all in the best of health. I might just mention that I have had no letters or cards from anyone since I wrote you. So it looks as if there was a stoppage in the mail again somewhere. Well Maggie I have just been wondering if the owners of the Rubislaw are paying you the full amount according to what we understand here the Captains wives were to receive £2-10 & 5/6 for each child Chief Engineers wives £2 & 5/6 for each child & so on with Mates & Jun Engineers. In the letter I received from the B.O.T they said that arrangements had been made with the owners for you to receive the allowance payable under the recent revision of the Government Scheme for the payment of allowances to the dependents of seamen interned in Germany. Did Rina say how

---

David Tulloch gives a picture of one of the 'small businesses' in Ruhleben. He talks about a nest of mice they had found which had provided a nice treat for the ferrets. Where the ferrets came from he does not say, but they were kept to chase the rats out of their holes so that the dogs in the camp could then kill the rats. An enterprising group of prisoners then cured the skins of the rats and made tobacco pouches out of them. Tulloch tells his wife jokingly that he could get a nice lady's purse for her.

Another enterprising prisoner who called himself Mr W.H. Smith made a deal with a newsagent in Berlin. *The Times* continued to be sold in Germany throughout the war and this gentleman bought the old copies from the newsagent at a reduced price, and then sold them on to his fellow prisoners. As the war progressed there appears to have been much more contact with Berlin.

A fortnightly magazine called *In Ruhleben Camp* was produced. This was subsequently upgraded to a larger, more elaborate production called *The Ruhleben Camp Magazine*. Many of the men had

contacts in Germany and it was published by a printer in Berlin. The magazine was a means of letting everyone know what was going on in the camp, but its facetious humour and jokey adverts helped to lift the men's spirits and to unite them.

But Ruhleben is perhaps best remembered today for its intellectual and cultural life. The academics in the camp set up the Arts & Science Union. They developed a programme of lectures of a very high standard covering a range of subjects. Less intellectual were the clubs known as 'Circles' and there were a number of these, including a Nautical Circle. In London, a committee had been set up by the Board of Trade to supply seamen interned abroad with text books to further their knowledge, particularly in marine engineering, and to prepare them for the appropriate grade examinations as soon as they were released.

A Camp School was soon set up, and a wide variety of subjects was offered at all levels, unlike the Arts & Science Union where the classes were more at university level. Classes in the Camp School were nevertheless of a high standard and Ruhleben became a centre for the examinations of, for example, the University of London, the London Chamber of Commerce, the Royal Society of Arts. Languages were very popular, and David Tulloch attended German classes. He has notes on German spelling and writing in his notebook.

Many of the prisoners had brought books with them. But more were needed, and in November 1915 the British Board of Education appealed for books of an educational nature or for money to buy books to be sent to Ruhleben. At this point there was both the Camp School and the Arts & Science Union in Ruhleben with 1,500 enrolled students and 150 lecturers and teachers. Over 5,000 books were sent, and this was supplemented by books belonging to the men themselves and by books requested by the prisoners for specific courses.

More books were sent to Ruhleben than to any other camp. For some time after the war ended, books could still be picked up in second-hand book-shops in Berlin with signatures of Ruhleben

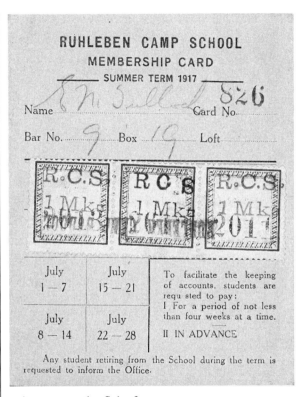

prisoners on the flyleaf.

As well as courses in languages and sciences, in technical subjects, in navigation and in commercial subjects, there was also a handicrafts department where the men could learn bookbinding, printing, leatherwork and silverwork. That all these were on offer reflects the wealth of talent among the men who had been imprisoned. Many men took advantage of these opportunities to learn something they had never tried before. David Tulloch took leatherwork classes, as well as German. But even those who didn't want to learn something new could find plenty to do in attending concerts and plays or watching sports.

There were so many lectures available that it was becoming difficult to find classrooms, but this was soon overcome with the help of the military authorities who gave permission to use parts of the camp which had up to then been closed to the prisoners. Joseph Powell, the camp commander, speculates whether they did this because it made it easier to govern the camp, or because they genuinely respected what the prisoners were doing. He feels that thanks to the attitude of the Germans, the prisoners were able to transform Ruhleben into a passable imitation of a university town.

This is not to say that life at Ruhleben was like a holiday camp. Although conditions improved, the men were still living in horse boxes and had to contend with the cold, the lack of privacy, inadequate sanitary facilities and insufficient food. And there was the constant worry about the families at home and how they were coping, both emotionally and financially. In a letter to his wife written in November 1917, David Tulloch worries that the owners of the *Rubislaw* are not paying her the full amount according to the revised government scheme for the payment of allowances to the dependents of seamen interned in Germany. He had asked Robert Cameron, the second engineer of the *Rubislaw*, to send for a copy of this revised scheme. Margaret Tulloch's allowance had just been increased to nineteen shillings and sixpence, but according to her husband's reckoning, a chief engineer's wife should be getting two pounds ten shillings plus two shillings and sixpence for each child. He had been in touch with the Board of Trade who had assured him that r eight young ones about 6 weeks ago. They were a nice tasty bit for the Ferrets. Oh Yes we have 6 or 8 Ferrets in Ruhleben, they are used for chasing rats out of holes + then the dogs does the rest. There are a gang of fellows who have taken on that job just for a bit of sport. They cure the Skins + the Camp School makes tobacco pouches etc out of them. I was thinking about asking them to make me a nice ladys purse for you, eh, you don't want it. Oh well I need not bother asking them. I see by your letter of the 10th of Oct which is the last one I received that you were anxious for my next letter to see how Ber 9 came off in the exchange. That we don't know yet for everything seems to be at a stand still again except for an occasional rumour that everything is settled + will be carried out this month. When the time does come; if ever it does, they won't get long notice, + know body can tell who is in the lucky 400. as it will be kept dark until the last minute. You also mention about the Xmas Parcels. Well I don't want you to send

arrangements had been made with the owners of the *Rubislaw* for her to receive the correct allowance.

In the same letter he talks about the rumours of possible release of some of the prisoners, and wonders who will be in the "lucky 400" and when it will happen. A couple of months later some 370 seamen were released, including some of the *Rubislaw*'s crew members, but David Tulloch was not among them. He had to wait for another 11 months.

Towards the end of 1918 in Germany there was a period of civil unrest. Germany had lost the war, her people were starving. A republic was proclaimed on 9 November, and the Kaiser, Wilhelm II, abdicated and fled the country. The Armistice was signed on 11 November, and the men of Ruhleben were free. Free to leave the camp and visit Berlin, but not yet in a position to leave Germany until arrangements were made. It was 21 November before the railway carriages arrived for the first stage of their journey home. As they left, each man was handed a letter from the Soldiers' Council. The letter blamed the war on the previous regime and

ENCLISHMEN!
Brothers from over the Channel.

It is tragic, deeply tragical, that a million dead on both sides were neeessary in order to bring home to us that after all we are brothers, & members of the same race. Have Germans & British ever, until now, torn each other to pieces ? From impressions gained in eompetent eireles yesterday, it is our personal opinion that your release is only a matter of days. When you are at home again, let it be your task to make known that the German people, in spite of all its vietories, still retained sufficient strength to take its destiny into its own hand & this time to keep it there. Let your aim be to make known that the German people, in this, its time of greatest need, whieh is also the proudest period of its history, instinetively easts its eyes across the water, looking for help. Englishmen! the German nation is proud, it will never beg, rather would it go to ruin. Brothers, or men from aeross the sea, the German people, left entirely to itself will eventually - there can be no doubt of this, - reeover from its wounds & regain its greatness. Draw the eonsequences from our words & aet aeeordingly when you are baek at home. Soldiers Couneil, Engländerlager, RUHLEBEN.
(signed) Zirwes. Kieser, Plümer, Wolff, Beer, Schütze.

urged the men not to leave with ill-feeling or hatred towards Germany, nor to hold the German people responsible for the deeds committed by the former autocratic leaders.

This new republic accepted that the men had suffered, but felt that the German population had suffered more. The men in Ruhleben had been amply provided for by the British government, but the German people were starving, and they warned against continuing to block the supply of food since this would only drive people to terrorism.

In one paragraph they say:

You are leaving the camp with your heads high, bound for freedom and home. History will record the years you have spent in the camp, and how you have bravely borne your captivity. Freedom and all it means follow four years of privations and sorrows. We congratulate you on your bearing, that nothing ever broke your spirit, or made you lose faith.

Unlike Charles Wilson, David Tulloch bore no ill will towards the Germans, and had happier memories of his time in Ruhleben, memories which he shared with his family when he returned to Aberdeen in December 1918. Many years later, at the age of 91, he wrote to one of his granddaughters, a long letter in which he goes into great detail about his life and about the value of education and what it had done for him.

At the very end of the letter, he writes: "I forgot to mention the four years and three months I was a

Prisoner of War in Germany". That was a part of his education, a part of his life he had learned from, but it was not something that preyed on his mind or overshadowed the rest of his life.

David Tulloch was also a regular member of the *Rubislaw*'s crew, he had been backwards and forwards to Germany many times, spoke and understood some German, and had many friends in Hamburg. In addition, he had been much more involved in the life of the camp than Charles Wilson had.

Like many of the prisoners he had gained something from his time in Ruhleben. It was here that he had found his love of gardening, something which stayed with him all his life and which he was able to share with his children and grandchildren.

David Tulloch

Gardening

DOREEN BLACK writes:

When the crew of the *Rubislaw* arrived at Ruhleben race course near Spandau on 6 November 1914 they would have seen an abandoned trotting race track and brick stable blocks set amidst a bleak, flat, winter landscape near the River Spree and the smoking chimneys of Berlin six miles away.

Did they feel relief that they had left behind the rotting hulks on the Elbe or dismay that they were exchanging one damp, dirty rat-infested environment for another? In the early 1900s Ruhleben was a popular destination for families enjoying a day out from the city, with its three grandstands, a restaurant, a clubhouse and a casino as well as the oval trotting track.

That November, Ruhleben was "a barren windswept desolate plain". When the last internees left four years later, the cultivable areas around the camp, the race track and the area within it had all been transformed. The Gardeners of Ruhleben deserve to be remembered. Theirs is a story of hope in adversity, of cooperation, of organisation, of imag-

View of Ruhleben camp in the snow.

ination and of hard physical work.

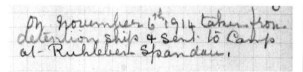

The bleak landscape, the barbed wire and the mud were not encouraging and in the first months of captivity the near starvation rations of putrid soup and black bread made life very difficult. The focus was on coping with the overcrowding, the cold, the damp, the rats and the hunger.

David Tulloch kept a little black notebook in which he wrote from time to time. Understandably, the first entries are all about food and, eventually, there are entries describing the weather and the joy of receiving parcels from home.

One detainee describes the weather on 8 January 1915 as "raining and blowing hard, grounds in horrible condition". On 16 January the weather was still bad and it snowed again on 28 February. Even when Spring came it was very wet and the camp became a sea of mud under the tread of thousands of men. The Germans had planned on receiving 1,500 prisoners but, at its peak, the camp housed around 4,500.

The camp's proximity to Berlin and the fact that this was a civilian internment camp meant that visitors from neutral countries could be allowed in. When Powell, the camp leader, invited the American Ambassador James W. Gerard to visit on 3 March 1915, he was horrified by what he saw.

One of his achievements was to persuade the German authorities to supply some wood to help improve conditions indoors and out. The lofts were made safer and, after some prisoners who were engineers improved the drainage, raised wooden pathways were laid. Permission was also given to use the racecourse.

March 28th Race course opened for football.

Some internees had started to create small gardens in biscuit tins and to grow shrubs to hide the barbed wire. By the summer of 1915 small gardens started to appear around the barracks and the prisoners were encouraged to improve the look of the camp. Israel Cohen writes about that summer in *The Ruhleben Prison Camp* 1917. "The joys of summer were made a little real by the pretty flower-bed that we planted around and opposite our barracks, and by the biscuit-tins filled with pansies, violets and bluebell that were suspended along the side of the wood staircase. The cost of these floral decorations was borne by the inmates of each barrack, whilst the gardening was done voluntarily by experts and amateurs." Joseph Powell, Camp Captain, writes, "The idea of having gardens originated with the gardeners interned in the camp".

Another important visitor to the camp was the Crown Princess Margaret of Sweden, formerly Princess Margaret of Connaught, (1882-1920) a granddaughter of Queen Victoria and wife of Crown Prince Gustav Adolf of Sweden. Prince Gustav, a keen botanist, later became an honorary member of the Royal Horticultural Society (RHS). The Crown Princess and her husband were given Sofiero Palace as a wedding gift and they spent their summers there creating gardens in the English style. Gustav's particular interest lay in rhododendrons.

Princess Margaret was concerned about the plight of prisoners of war in camps in Europe, particularly British prisoners. In 1916 she visited Ruhleben and brought a gift of seeds. This created a further interest in gardening and the Ruhleben Horticultural Society (RuhHS) was formed. The first meeting was held on 25 September 1916 and by the end of the year there were over 400 members. The society's aim was to promote knowledge of horticulture through lectures and practical gardening.

On 30 September a letter from Thomas Howat, the secretary, arrived at the headquarters of the RHS in Vincent Square in London. Howat asked

Absender: Engländerlager Ruhleben

Thomas Howat,

Baracke   5
Box   13   30th. September 1916.

An —To M Royal Horticultural Society, London.
                                        Ort

                              -Straße No.

GELD IST AN INTERNIERTE PERSÖNLICH ZU SENDEN | MONEY TO BE SENT BY POSTAL ORDER
UND ZWAR AUSSCHLIESSLICH DURCH POSTANWEISUNG. | ONLY, NOT PER REGISTERED LETTER. —
— AUF DER RÜCKSEITE DES ABSCHNITTES IST DER | ADDRESSEE'S FULL NAME MUST BE WRIT-
VOLLE NAME DES EMPFÄNGERS ZU WIEDERHOLEN. | TEN LEGIBLY ON COUNTERFOIL SLIP.

Gentlemen,

        I have been instructed by my Committee to
inform you,that on Monday 25th.September 1916 a
Horticultural Society was formed With the title
"Ruhleben Horticultural Society"the aims of this
society being to cultivate and beautify the ground
around the barracks and public thoroughfares in the
Lager,and to further the knowledge of horticulture.

We desire to become affiliated to the Royal Horticultural Society.Under the circumstances in which we
are presently situated we are unable of course to
remit the usual fee but trust this will be no hindrance to our enjoying the privileges of affiliation.
[Certainly not. W.W. Wr. R.H.S.]
        It may interest the members of your Society
to know that gardening started immediately after our
internment in the Camp and since then has steadily
increased.During this,our second summer,the magnificent
show of flowers and tasteful decorative schemes which
were carried out have done much to alleviate our lot.

Although the individual efforts of our barrack gardeners
have been very satisfactory we nevertheless feel,that
as a Society we shall have greater scope and receive n
more support.

        As the work we have in view is a large one
we should be very grateful for gifts of bulbs and
seeds.

        Thanking you in anticipation,

            I remain,Gentlemen,

                Yours faithfully,

                    Howat

                    Secry.

for the Ruhleben group to be affiliated to the RHS. "Under the circumstances," he states, "we are unable to remit the usual fee but trust this will be no hindrance to our enjoying the privileges of affiliation". In his letter we can see, written in red pen by the secretary of the RHS in London, the words, "absolutely not". No payment was required. Howat also writes, "we should be grateful for gifts of bulbs and seeds".

The RHS was, and is, the UK's leading gardening charity "dedicated to advancing horticulture and promoting good gardening".

The RuhHS became affiliated to the RHS on 12 December 1916. There were 50 members at first; by the end of that year there were 454. In September 1917, there were 943 members, almost a quarter of the camp population.

The first committee consisted of the following: Thomas Howat, Secretary & Treasurer (Glasgow); L.P. Warner, President & Chairman (Mansfield-Woodhouse); Leonard P. Roberts, Vice Chairman (Dorking), formerly a woodwork instructor;

The Ruhleben Horticultural Society Committee, Germany. 1917. Sitting [left to right] – J.M. Dickson (Edinburgh); Thomas Howat, Secretary & Treasurer (Glasgow); L.P. Warner, President and Chairman, (Mansfield-Woodhouse); Leonard P. Roberts, Vice-Chairman (Dorking); Geo A. Wyllie (Aberdeen). Standing – I. Lazarus (London); Alfred Hill (Aberdeen); Wm Moll (London); J. Blackburn (Huddersfield); Wm Cayley (Cardiff); W.R. Cooper (Nottingham); B. Cooper (Coventry); Wm Harris (Reading).

J.M. Dickson (Edinburgh), a graduate of Edinburgh University with a B.Sc. in Agriculture; Alfred Hill BSc and BSc Agriculture, a former assistant in Agricultural Chemistry at the University of Aberdeen and a teacher, who was arrested in Berlin; George Wyllie (Aberdeen); I. Lazarus (London); William Moll (London); J. Blackburn (Huddersfield); William Cayley (Cardiff); W.R. Cooper (Nottingham); B. Cooper (Coventry) and William Harris (Reading). Of the committee of 13, four were Scots, two of whom were from Aberdeen.

In a letter received in London on 20 December 1916 Howat acknowledges the affiliation. He is very grateful for the bulbs and seeds which have arrived and been planted and for the six pamphlets on gardening matters. The RHS had a proud history of charitable work in World War I and in 1917 sent out six cases and one parcel of seeds and bulbs; also six pamphlets of instructions.

At home an appeal was made for seeds and tubers. Among those who generously agreed to provide seeds were Suttons, Carters, Barr & Sons, Kelways, and William Smith & Sons of Aberdeen, which was owned by the Wyllie family. The eldest son, George Wyllie, born 1893, was destined to follow his father in the business. He was sent to Germany to study seed growing and processing with the firm of Ernst Benary. In 1914 he was captured and sent to Ruhleben where he remained till the end of the war. Unfortunately he contracted tuberculosis in the camp and his health deteriorated after his release. He was treated in the Tor na Dee Sanatorium near Aberdeen where he died in 1932.

When David Tulloch retired to Aberdeen he always bought his seed potatoes and seeds from Smiths.

Individuals also rallied to the appeal for seeds and in appreciation, Howat sent them RHS membership cards as keepsakes.

Throughout the rest of the war, the RHS sent out seeds and tubers and received back from Ruhleben copies of the lecture syllabus, membership cards, committee minutes, vegetable planting plans, lists of flower varieties and high quality photographs showing the Barrack and Public Gardens, the Nursery Garden, the Market Garden, the flower and vegetable shows, the greenhouses and boiler system, etc. These papers and photographs are carefully preserved in the RHS archive at the Lindley Library and provide a fascinating record of the development of the gardening in the camp.

Membership of the RuhHS was open to all and David Tulloch became a member in 1916, paying the one mark membership fee. A collection of reading materials was available to members and lectures were held every two weeks during the winter

RUHLEBEN 1917.
PART OF BRR 9 GARDEN.

1190

Photo of garden outside Barrack 9 (David Tulloch's barrack).

months. Subjects included: How to grow melons, how to grow fruit, and technical advice on improving the nitrogen content in soil.

The earliest efforts had been to disguise the barbed wire and enhance the areas around the barracks. Now there was a comprehensive list of those responsible for keeping the gardens – and prizes for the best kept ones. Barrack 8, known as the Sailors Barrack, had a lovely rose bed. David Tulloch was in Barrack 9 Box 19.

Barrack 3 garden in July 1917.

Barrack 12

In 1917 records show that there were 22 men responsible for the Barrack Gardens, and there are photographs showing the variety of the planting and design. The Public Gardens, cared for by 16 men, comprised the Tea House Garden, Triangular Garden, Terrace Gardens, Promenade Gardens, Y.M.C.A. and A.S.E. Gardens, Trafalgar Square, Carpenter's Shop, Captain's Office, Phoenix Club, Wash House Border and Rock Garden. In the winter of 1917, 150 trees and shrubs were transplanted from around the racecourse into the camp.

Behind Barrack 10, 600 square yards were cultivated to make a Nursery Garden. Old packing cases, biscuit crates and tobacco boxes were recycled with great ingenuity and glass was purchased to make cold frames and a greenhouse. The plan of the nursery and surroundings reveals a tool shed, a sorting and packing shed, a workshop, a boiler house and cold frames. There was a range of expertise in the camp, and men with skills in engineering, joinery, gardening and design put their experience to good use.

Nursery showing greenhouse and frames.

In the RuhHS report 1917-18 there is a list of the 20 men working in the nursery area. C.H.G. Gibson of Saltburn, Yorkshire, is the supervisor in charge of six men whose job it is to create and erect frames, supports, cold frames, window boxes, rustic arches, staging and glass houses. Ingenuity and recycling were the order of the day. One of the men listed is G. Robertson from Inverurie and two others are from Edinburgh, including J. Dickson.

There are four men in charge of the heating

One of the melon frames. These 'Sutton's Ringleader', weighed 3¼ lbs each. © RHS LINDLEY COLLECTIONS

installation which, by 1918, makes a big difference to production. After vegetable and flower seedlings had been planted out in the flower beds, Barrack gardens and market garden, the cold frames were used to grow melons, pumpkins and cucumbers. Tomatoes were grown on in the greenhouse. The six men in charge of growing plants under glass include J. Dickson again, and George Wyllie, whose expertise in seed growing must have been invaluable. Lastly, three men work outside in the nursery garden itself. All men are listed alongside the name of their home town.

On 12 January 1917 the RuhHS is given permission to rent five acres of ground at £5 per month in which to cultivate a vegetable garden. This area took up almost half the internal oval of the racetrack around the pond. The other half remained a sports field. A grant of 3,517.85 Marks was given by the captains' committee to cover costs of equipment and manure. This sum was repaid by the end of 1917 due to the success of the enterprise.

Although there were a few professional gardeners in the camp, many men were needed to create and

The Vegetable Garden, showing the scale of the enterprise and the area cultivated.

maintain the Vegetable or Market Garden. Three to five feet of sand had to be removed from the ground before they could grow vegetables. There were 10 prisoner volunteers and another 18 prisoners were employed by the society to manually dig out this sand and reveal the earth beneath. David Tulloch's name is on this list. Any money earned could be sent home to the family. Added to the soil were 30 loads of rather poor pig manure, as was slag, bone-meal and potash.

The Vegetable Garden was first planted in April 1917. This was production on a large scale requiring expert organisation and manpower. R.G. Buckley, described as the Field Manager, is given

Plan of vegetable garden 1917. © RHS LINDLEY COLLECTIONS

much of the credit for the success of the enterprise. There are three Plot Supervisors and 26 staff listed.

David Tulloch's name appears on this list also. David was born on a croft in Morayshire in 1875, one of 15 children, and left school at 12 years of age to work on farms until his later teens when he followed in the footsteps of his elder brother and moved to Aberdeen. He trained as an engineer in A. Hall & Co. and joined the Merchant Navy gaining his Chief Engineer's certificate in 1902. He, therefore, had some agricultural experience in his early years and, although only five foot four inches tall, he was very strong and fit. At the age of 93 he was still keeping a large and immaculate vegetable garden in Aberdeen.

The letter sent to Lord Provost Taggart wishing the Citizens of Aberdeen a prosperous New Year and published in the *Evening Express* of 5 January 1915 contains 16 signatures, including those of George Wyllie and Alfred Hill BSc. David Tulloch's signature indicates that he is the sender. It can be seen from this 1914 list of names that Hill, Wyllie and

Sweet peas: The seed for the exhibits was presented by Wm. Smith & Son, Aberdeen.

Tulloch had known each other then and, interestingly, in 1917, their names all appear on the vegetable gardening staff lists.

It seems strange to us that the internees first grew flowers and only later started to grow vegetables. Indeed there was a split in the committee when there was a proposal to grow vegetables.

There was obviously a deep-seated desire to improve the melancholy of the camp surroundings, but the need for fresh vegetables to supplement their meagre diet could not be denied. The situation in Germany may also have had an effect, as frost killed the potato crop in 1916-17 and food shortages led to rioting. Fresh vegetables would be very welcome.

The vegetable display at the show in 1917.

The RuhHS held bulb, flower and vegetable shows in the camp using RHS guidance and rules. A bulb show was held on 7 April 1917 in the Y.M.C.A. hall and a Summer Flower Show, which included vegetables, was held on 3–4 August. There were 61 varieties of flowers grown from seed and 22 flowering plants grown from cuttings, most of which were exhibited. There were 102 entries in 11 classes and 1,400 plants were displayed.

Some German officers and dignitaries from a Netherlands delegation visited the show. Sales of plants and produce boosted the show balance sheet as 487.55 Marks was made and costs only came to 129.85 Marks. A healthy profit by anyone's standards!

It is incredible to read that they grew 83 varieties of sweet peas. These especially must have brought back fond memories of gardens at home. Interestingly, in amongst the sweet peas exhibit is a notice acknowledging that the seeds were supplied by W. Smith & Sons, Aberdeen, George Wyllie's family firm. We can see in the photographs that the exhibits are displayed on staging just as you would have seen at the Chelsea and RHS shows of the day.

Varieties of 14 vegetables are exhibited with an acknowledgement that the seeds were supplied by the RHS London. Only one variety of potato, 'Factor', was shown and thereafter there is no other mention of a potato crop. Perhaps this was because the German potato crop had been very poor in 1916-17 due to late frost.

In September 1917, within a year of its inception, the RuhHS report sent to London states that a nursery has been created with cold frames and a greenhouse, and that there is now a vegetable garden. There have been lectures, and an impressive 20,000 bedding plant seedlings and 23,000 vegetable seedlings have been raised and planted out. Vegetables have been sold to the canteen and the finances of the RuhHS are strong.

Gardening is never straightforward and so it was in the camp. Pests and diseases, shortages and unpredictable weather had to be coped with.

The weather here has been very unsettled & not at all like Summer. I can't remember if I told you that I had a P.C. from Miss Beatie, so you can thank her for me. I have had no mail since I wrote to Maggie last week, they seem to have got hung up again somewhere. I had a box of Oat Cakes from Amy last week, & some treacle biscuits, & by jove they were a treat. I never thought it possible to enjoy oat cakes so much as I enjoyed these. What surprises me is that they keep so well for such a long time. We get the Danish bread regular every week, it is very good bread but doesn't keep very long, by the end of the week it is generally mouldy. ████████ What like is your potato crop? Surely the worm won't take them. We put out a lot of young plants last Saturday, & today I had a look at them & found dozens completely gone with the Surface Caterpillar. It is not very large but can do a terrible lot of damage, in most cases I found him by the plant.

Caterpillars, aphids, diamond-backed moths, wire worms, cockchafer grubs and turnip flea beetle are reported. There was a pond in the area of the Market Garden and the sound of frogs and toads kept prisoners awake. Hopefully these noisy inhabitants fed on some of the pests affecting the crops. In one of his letters to his wife, Maggie, David asks how her allotment in Aberdeen is doing and complains about pests eating the camp crops:

"The weather here has been unsettled and not at all like Summer… What like is your potato crop? Surely the worm won't take them. We put in a lot of young plants last Saturday and today I had a look at them and found dozens completely gone with the Surface Caterpillar. It is not very large but can do a terrible lot of damage, in most cases I found him by the plant."

When there were shortages of watering cans and plant pots, the Prisoner's Aid Committee in Berlin donated 1,600 terracotta pots. Manure had to be

◀ David's letter showing some content has been censored.

sourced and tea leaves were used to fertilize the Barrack Gardens.

David writes to his wife in 31 July 1918 from Ruhleben complaining about the weather: "We are badly wanting a few weeks sunshine to ripen the tomatoes," (a crop he never attempted to grow in Aberdeen as he only had a cold frame).

We are badly wanting a few weeks sunshine to ripen the Tomatoes.

Berlin winters were harsh with plenty frost and snow, and in summer there could be drought. The strong winds which swept across the flat landscape created sandstorms which disrupted many seedlings. Parts of the grounds were stony. We know that boulders dug out of the Market Garden area were used to create the Rock Garden, which improved an unsightly area in the camp beside the wash house. In general, the soil was described as "dry, loose, dirty sand which rain quickly transforms into mud".

There was an attempt to keep bees, but the bee population became infected and the enterprise was not successful.

Reports sent back to RHS in London show that by May 1918 a pithouse has been erected, that the greenhouse has been extended and now includes a forcing house, a cool house and an intermediate house. The area under glass had been extended from 500 to 1,400 square feet and a heating system had been installed.

James Blackburn who was a RuhHS committee member was a master gardener from a Huddersfield family of nurserymen. He had been working as an orchid grower for Curt Moll, a family friend, in Borgsdorf when war broke out. The Moll family owned extensive glasshouses and Herr Moll helped with equipment for building the greenhouses and the heating system.

In August 1914 he was tending to the boilers whilst Herr Moll was on holiday. His commitment to his task cost him dear: he missed the last train which would have allowed him to leave Berlin and was captured. Although Blackburn was interned in

Interior of the Nursery Pithouse and staff.

Ruhleben he was, at the request of Curt Moll, allowed a daily pass which enabled him to keep working for the firm and he managed to bring in some food for the internees.

In 1917 Blackburn used his contacts in Berlin to help him source a second-hand boiler. Although men had to get up during the night to tend the boiler, a heated greenhouse made a huge difference to production levels. With hothouses, pot plants and cut flowers were available even in winter.

Sadly, after the war, Blackburn was considered by some to have worked with the Germans and his contribution to feeding the prisoners was forgotten. After his release he kept up his close friendship with the Moll family but, in World War II, his own carnation houses were requisitioned, never used and neglected... a loss from which he never recovered.

Herr Moll's greenhouses were destroyed during the advance on Berlin at the end of World War II and he committed suicide.

The report also itemises the vegetables sold at the canteen and the prices charged. For example, between May 1917 and March 1918, 11,997 bundles of radishes, 2,450 celery, 1,661 leeks and 7,259 beets were sold. Receipts from the vegetable sales at the canteen during this period were 8,982.85 Marks.

There was such demand for fresh vegetables that rationing was introduced for certain varieties in short supply and 2,332 vegetable cards were issued. The card shown for season 1918-1919 entitled the

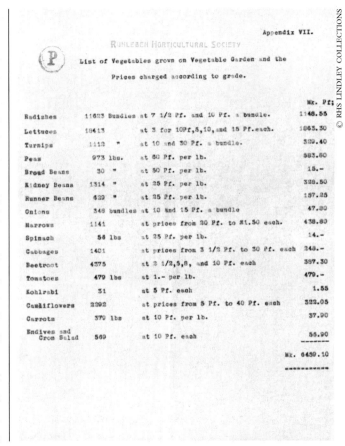

Appendix VII.

RUHLEBEN HORTICULTURAL SOCIETY

List of Vegetables grown on Vegetable Garden and the
Prices charged according to grade.

			Mk. Pf;
Radishes	11623 Bundles	at 7 1/2 Pf. and 10 Pf. a bundle.	1148.55
Lettuces	18413	at 3 for 10Pf,5,10,and 15 Pf. each.	1863.30
Turnips	1113 "	at 10 and 30 Pf. a bundle.	339.40
Peas	973 lbs.	at 60 Pf. per lb.	583.60
Broad Beans	30 "	at 50 Pf. per lb.	15.-
Kidney Beans	1314 "	at 25 Pf. per lb.	328.50
Runner Beans	629 "	at 25 Pf. per lb.	157.25
Onions	348 bundles	at 10 and 15 Pf. a bundle	47.80
Marrows	1141	at prices from 30 Pf. to M1.50 each.	438.80
Spinach	56 lbs	at 25 Pf. per lb.	14.-
Cabbages	1401	at prices from 3 1/2 Pf. to 30 Pf. each	348.-
Beetroot	4375	at 2 1/2,5,8, and 10 Pf. each	397.30
Tomatoes	479 lbs	at 1.- per lb.	479.-
Kohlrabi	31	at 5 Pf. each	1.55
Cauliflowers	2392	at prices from 5 Pf. to 40 Pf. each	322.05
Carrots	379 lbs	at 10 Pf. per lb.	37.90
Endives and Cron Salad	569	at 10 Pf. each	55.90
			Mk. 6459.10

I praise the Tender Flower,
That on a mournful day
Bloomed in my garden bower
And made the winter gay.

Robert Bridges

Spring bulb show 1918 with Robert Bridges poem displayed.

bearer to cabbages red, green and savoy, a marrow, one lot of leeks, one lot of celery, one lot of kale, one lot of sprouts and one pound of tomatoes.

A small exhibition of spring bulbs was held in January 1918. The pots are beautifully arranged on a two-tier staging and displayed on the backdrop is the Robert Bridges poem, *"I Praise The Tender Flower"*. At the Spring Flower Show held at Easter 1918, some 600 pots were shown and 2,000 were sold, as well as cut flowers. Spring flowers must have cheered the prisoners who saw some of their friends being released whilst they were left behind.

Celery trenches in the market garden.

In June 1918 a testimonial sent to the RHS in London has the following words written over a sweet pea design:

"We the committee and members of the Ruhleben Horticultural Society desire to express to the RHS London and friends at home our heartiest thanks for the valued gift and generous support, which have made possible our work in Ruhleben. We request the acceptance of this testimonial as a token of our gratitude and appreciation."

The testimonial was designed by William Powell and beautifully decorated with a hanging basket, cream thistle and Tudor rose design. At the foot is a watercolour illustration of the Barrack Gardens and the Market Garden with men at work beside the pond.

Membership of the RuhHS had grown to well over 900 at its peak in 1917. Members came from all parts of Britain and the Empire, and from all walks of life, but during 1918, membership fell. The population of the camp had been reduced to about a half due to releases. Some prisoners may have anticipated that the war was drawing to its end, but there were plenty internees involved in gardening.

Prizewinning promenade bed with tennis courts and market garden in the distance.

By the end of the war the camp was pretty well self sufficient in vegetables and the prisoners were faring better than the starving Berliners. At the time of writing its report in April 1918 the RuhHS states that preparations are in hand to grow 33,000 lettuces, 18,000 bunches of radishes, 16,000 leeks, 2,000 tomato plants and 250 marrows. Of the 8,000 lettuce seedlings that had been raised, half had been planted out.

Some bulbs were now being purchased from Holland and there were Spring flowers in the gardens around the camp – "the early yellow crocuses

shortage of plant pots had been alleviated.

The report for 1918-1919 was never written, as the prisoners were released in November 1918. We can only imagine their feelings when they realised they were going home and would see their loved ones for the first time in four years and four months. Their gardening activities must have contributed both to their physical health and to their mental wellbeing.

We know of one internee, David Tulloch, who continued to grow beautiful flowers and vegetables for another 50 years, passing his love of gardening on to his children. Two of his great-grandchildren are keen gardeners. One great-granddaughter is a garden designer and one great-grandson has an allotment.

Now some of his great-great-grandchildren enjoy helping in the allotment. David's experience in the camp was harsh, but the knowledge he gained has been passed on to future generations in a way he and the gardeners of Ruhleben could never have imagined.

and the scarlet Duc van Thois have been particularly beautiful" – according to the report. The Rock Garden which was beside the wash house merits a "particular mention for having redeemed one of the most melancholy views in camp". By May, 15,000 bedding plants would be ready to plant out and the

The Crew and Passengers Return

The *Rubislaw*'s manifest in July 1914 lists all the crew as prisoners of war, and gives the date of their release. It shows that most of the men were in Ruhleben until the end of the war in 1918. But a few were repatriated before then on the grounds of age or of ill health.

The first to come home was the ship's captain, Thomas Walker, who was 60 at the time the *Rubislaw* sailed into Hamburg. His health had suffered as a result of his internment, mainly due to the lack of nourishing food, and he spent the last six months of his captivity in the Charlottenburg sanatorium in Berlin. When he was repatriated 14 months after his internment he had lost three stones in weight.

As a result of an exchange of prisoners, Captain Walker was able to leave Germany on Friday, 15 October 1915. Forty other prisoners had been released at the same time. He was accompanied by a military escort to Bentheim, some 500 miles from Berlin, and then through Holland to Flushing, where he joined the mail boat to London. On his arrival in Aberdeen on 19 October, he gave an interview to the press and described conditions in the camp.

He reported that there was no brutal treatment in the camp, and that the remaining members of the crew were fairly well and in good spirits. They saw each other every day. However, sanitary arrangements were very bad, there was a lot of sickness, and as winter approached, things would get worse. Food was in very short supply and what there was was wholly inadequate.

A couple of months later three more members of the crew were released, this time on the grounds of age. Charles Wilson left Ruhleben on Christmas Eve 1915 after 17 months internment there. With him were James Cummings, the second mate, and an able seaman, Frank Johnston, both men in their fifties. According to the *Aberdeen Daily Journal* of 27 December 1915, that left 14 of the crew "still in durance vile, but nevertheless by no means downhearted, and looking forward to a speedy termination of their exile from bonnie Aiberdeen." Charles Wilson looked "hale and hearty, notwith-

S.S. RUBISLAW CREW IN GERMAN CAMP.

CAPTAIN WALKER RETURNS TO ABERDEEN.

PRISONER FOR 14 MONTHS.

Captain Thomas Walker, of the s.s. Rubislaw, who has been interned in Germany for 14½ months, was recently exchanged with other prisoners of war, and has returned to Aberdeen.

On account of the privations he underwent, particularly through the insufficiency of food, the health of Captain Walker completely broke down, and for the last six months he was in a sanatorium just outside Berlin. He is now, fortunately, recovering, although he lost as much as three stones in weight. The internment camp at Ruhleben is only seven miles from Berlin, and there are 5000 men at present there. Captain Walker visited the camp on Friday night and bade good-bye to his crew, who looked fairly well and in good spirits.

It was on the 31st July last year that the s.s. Rubislaw sailed from Aberdeen on her usual voyage to Hamburg. She carried 18 of a crew and 9 passengers. They arrived on Sunday,

Aberdeen Daily Journal, Wednesday, 20 October 1915

standing his trying ordeal and made no secret of his joy at being back again with his wife and family in Aberdeen".

His granddaughter, Nan, says that Charles Wilson never spoke of his experiences. The only thing she remembers him saying was: "If I ever see a German I will fell him to the ground." He would not have talked to his granddaughters about his time in Ruhleben, but did he perhaps speak to his sons? My grandfather was 27 at the outbreak of war, and in the Merchant Navy. Would his father perhaps have talked to him? Even if he did not, my grandfather would have been well aware of the effect internment had had on his father, and on the family at home.

In retrospect it does perhaps explain my grandfather's attitude when I left home to study at a German university for a year. He could not understand why I should do this and was obviously unhappy with my decision. Maybe he was remembering his father's experience of 50 years before.

More members of the crew of the *Rubislaw* were released before the end of the war. Alexander Inglis, then age 38, one of the firemen, was released on 6 August 1916 on the grounds of ill health. He had been in hospital in Berlin for about four months before his release and was admitted to the City Hospital in Aberdeen shortly after his return home. Inglis, who was married with seven of a family, wrote to the Aberdeen Prisoners of War Bureau, thanking them for the food parcels which he had received while in Ruhleben. Without them, he said, it would have been impossible for the prisoners to exist. The food they were given was "only fit for swine". He did concede, however, that the food given to the patients in hospital was much better, and that they were treated well.

Several of the crew were released before the end of hostilities, but not until early in 1918. Angus Leith, by then 53, another fireman, or 'donkeyman', was one of a group of some 300 prisoners over the age of 45 exchanged towards the end of the war, arriving home in January 1918. He, too, spoke appreciatively of the food parcels received from home.

A couple of months later, on 23 March 1918, two able seamen, William Bruce and Thomas Hughes, and fireman William Forbes, were also released.

The remaining members of the crew – first mate Thomas Pattison, chief engineer David Tulloch, second engineer Robert Cameron, fireman James Graham, able seaman James Baird, ordinary seamen Fred Bryce and James Shepherd, assistant steward Alexander Mackie, and George Barron the cook, were in Ruhleben until the end of hostilities.

And what of the five male passengers who had been on board the *Rubislaw*? Mr True had been able to leave Germany almost immediately, and Dr James Paterson had reached home on 6 November 1914. That left John Milne of the Aberdeen Commercial Company, James Craik of the Northern Agricultural Company and the medical student Alexander Garden.

John Milne returned home in September 1915 for reasons of ill-health, and as part of an exchange of prisoners. He reported that there were about 50

Die Kgl. Niederländische Gesandtschaft bescheinigt hierdurch, daß die aufgeklebte Photographie den Paß-inhaber darstellt und daß die Unterschrift unterhalb der Photographie von demselben eigenhändig vollzogen worden ist.

Berlin, den *12 Januar* 1918

David Tulloch's passport to freedom.

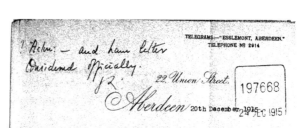

PRISONERS, &c. GERMANY.

1915.

20 December.

R Esslemont M.P., to Ld R. Cecil

No. 197668   File No. 76915

Received by

Last Paper 196686

(Subject.)

Ruhleben.

Ths. memo. prepared by Mr Jas Craik, released. Enquires whether anything can be done to facilitate exchange of ships boys and old seamen.

(Print.)

(Minutes.)

? reply that an agreement has been reached for the return prisoners over 55 & under 17 that we have proposed that

(How disposed of.)

TELEGRAMS:—"ESSLEMONT, ABERDEEN."
TELEPHONE No 2914

22, Union Street.
Aberdeen 20th December 1915

197668
24 DEC 1915

Lord Robert Cecil, M.P.
Foreign Office,
Downing Street,
London, S.W.

Dear Lord Robert,

I am sending you herewith a memorandum which has been submitted to me by one of my constituents, Mr James Craik, 7 Mile-end Avenue, Aberdeen, who has been a civil prisoner at Ruhleben since the outbreak of war.

It would be certainly a great matter if anything could be done for these young boys and old men. Perhaps you will let me know at your convenience whether you can do anything to facilitate exchanges.

Yours faithfully,

Ro R Esslemont

The correspondence generated by James Craik's letter to his MP in December 1915.

Aberdeen men at Ruhleben, most of them sailors. The men's last message to him had been: "Tell our people to keep on sending parcels".

James Craik returned home in December 1915, and immediately wrote to his Member of Parliament highlighting the plight of boys under 17 and men over 55 who were interned in Ruhleben, and asking if something could be done to repatriate them.

In his memorandum written on his return, Craik states that: "There are about 20 boys under 17 in the Camp all belonging to ships. They had been either apprentices or mess-room boys. The Camp is a very bad place for them, as they come into constant contact with the lower elements of the seafaring class who are apt to have a very unfavourable influence on them morally. In a Camp inhabited exclusively by men these boys are in danger of being ruined morally and physically by the evil influences to which they are subjected".

By this time, however, the authorities had already managed to obtain agreement for the release of boys and of men over 55.

ENGLÄNDERLAGER, RUHLEBEN, GERMANY.
XMAS, 1917.

With Best Wishes for Xmas & for 1918. from A. Garden

Unlike his fellow-passengers, John Milne and James Craik, Alexander Garden was in Ruhleben to the very end. *The Press & Journal* received a Christmas card from Ruhleben, signed by him, on 7 January 1918. Garden resumed his studies when he eventually returned to Aberdeen, and he graduated in 1924.

The Rubislaw after the War

Under the terms of the Armistice the S.S. *Rubislaw* was returned by Germany on 21 December 1918, but in a very dilapidated state. She had sustained considerable damage while being used by the Germans. After extensive repairs, she was finished and ready for use in March 1919. A Glasgow company chartered her from the owners and for the next two years she carried cargo between British and Mediterranean ports, returning to her home port of Aberdeen in March 1921.

It was expected that she would be laid up in port for some time, along with many other vessels, but in fact, less than a year later, in February 1922, she resumed her voyages to Germany, and for the first time since August 1914, she sailed once more into Hamburg. Reports in the press tell of the very warm welcome given to the ship and her crew, with everyone delighted to see them back. Several of her crew were those who had sailed on her in 1914, including David Tulloch, the chief engineer.

Captain Walker, however, was no longer captain. That position was filled by Thomas Pattison, who

The Rubislaw struck a mine in November 1939 and sank within minutes. Inset: Captain James Nicolson.

had been the *Rubislaw*'s first mate when she sailed into Hamburg in August 1914.

Sailings between Aberdeen and Hamburg continued right up until the start of World War II in the autumn of 1939. The *Rubislaw* did continue working after that, but on other routes. In November of that year she was carrying a cargo of cement from London to Aberdeen when she struck a mine off the south-east coast of England. She sank within two minutes. Fortunately a mine-sweeper operating nearby saw the incident, and was able to pick up four survivors. The remaining 13 crew members,

RUBISLAW
ABERDEEN
NICOLSON J.H., MASTER
BRUCE R.C.
CAMERON R.W.
HUNTER W.F.J.
IMLACH A.
MCREYNOLDS G.
MUNRO J.
PETRIE G.
PIRIE W.J.
RUSSELL A.D.
SIMPSON T.
SMART E.

The Tower Hill Memorial in London

including the captain, James Nicolson, were drowned. One of the men who died was the chief

engineer, Robert Cameron. He had been second engineer on the *Rubislaw* in 1914, and had spent four years in Ruhleben. Like many of his fellow crew members in 1914, he had rejoined the *Rubislaw* when she resumed sailing after the war.

When the ship struck the mine his watch had just ended and he had gone off duty. The second engineer who had taken over the watch was thrown into the ship's bilges by the explosion, but managed to fight his way to the surface and was one of the four who survived.

The names of the men who died are commemorated on the Tower Hill Memorial in London. This memorial was created by the Imperial War Graves Commission to remember merchant navy seamen and fishermen who were killed as a result of enemy action, and have no grave but the sea.

This story began when the *Rubislaw* was impounded by Germany on the first day of World War I, and finishes 25 years later when she was sunk by a German mine in the first months of World War II.

My Grandpa

DOREEN BLACK writes:

To anyone seeing my maternal grandfather David McKay Tulloch walking down an Aberdeen street, he would have seemed very ordinary. He would have worn a dark three-piece suit complete with gold watch and chain, a trilby hat, and would have carried a leather shopping bag, but to me he was special.

I knew that in his pocket would be a brown paper bag (in case we spotted any wild raspberries), a piece of twine and a pocket knife for emergencies, and

Granny and Grandpa in the garden.

Grandpa in his Anstruther garden wearing his waistcoat and hat.

that later, by the fire, he would tell me the most wonderful tales of his travels and experiences. He would teach me to knit, play games with me and show endless patience taking me to the park or the boating pond.

One of my earliest memories is of putting on a clover-coloured beret and mitts trimmed with brown velvet ribbon (knitted by Granny) and rushing over the footbridge in Cults, near Aberdeen, to meet my grandparents off the train. I must have been about three years old. This was a special day and, in all of my early life, teens and early twenties, they both played a significant role. I spent many childhood hours following Grandpa around the garden – 'helping' him and listening to his stories of his adventures in far-off lands… Germany, India, Africa, Russia…

Grandpa was small, yet very strong, handsome and quiet. He grew every vegetable and fruit and cultivated flowers of many varieties. He had an immaculate 'sheddie' in which his tools were stored and where he let his grandchildren use a vice, saws and hammers to create simple wooden boats to sail.

Doreen and her grandfather behind the strawberry bed.

Doreen holding a watering can in his Cairncry garden.

As well as knitting, he taught me about gardening, how to play cards (but never on a Sunday), how to fish (even with a walking stick, string and safety pin), where all the best wild raspberries and blaeberries were to be found.

He was always patient, tolerant and kind. People use the expression, "he never said a bad word about anyone". In Grandpa's case, this was true. He told us about his time in the internment camp in Germany, but never displayed any hatred or criticism of the German people, except for one particular guard who was universally disliked throughout the camp.

I was born in October 1945 in Fife. My parents lived with Granny and Grandpa in Anstruther. My father was a banker and my mother, a teacher until her marriage, worked for the Ministry of Food. It was only later that I realised how well the four had got on and, in fact, my father and his father-in-law were very close. They were in the ARP together and spent much time in each other's company.

After the war, my parents returned to Aberdeen, but childhood holidays were spent with my grandparents; when we moved to Glasgow this continued, as did their visits to us.

In 1956, we returned to Aberdeen. When my father died in 1962 at the age of 52, my grandparents were deeply upset. As Granny and Grandpa reached their nineties, my mother tended to her mother, now bedridden, every day and I helped. Grandpa, as a former seaman and internee, was resourceful. He could cook, too. He tended his garden and did daily household chores right up to the day he died, aged nearly 94.

David McKay Tulloch was born on 25 February 1875, the sixth of 15 children born to Alexander Tulloch and Jane Gow. His father is described as manager of a farm near Forres. The Gows were farmers at Pluscarden and it was in the Free Church Manse there that Alexander and Jane were married on 22 June 1866.

In 1881, the family moved to Cromdale in the Spey valley, between Grantown and Aberlour, and it was from there that Grandpa walked four miles to

My father and my grandfather (his father-in-law) were very close. Here, they are pictured in the ARP.

Deskie.
Glenlivet
Ballindalloch
28ᵗʰ Nov. 91

The bearer David Tulloch who has been in my employment for twelve months. I have always found to be an honest, careful & most intelligent young man, and does his work so pleasantly and actively that it is a pleasure to see him at it. He is much above the average of men of his years in anything & everything that he puts his hands to- and I have great pleasure in giving him this testimonial.

Geo Bennett

Letter of commendation in 1891 for the 16-year-old David from George Bennet, farmer, at Deskie.

school. He often told me that they could go to school only if they had boots and if there was a teacher. The Education Scotland Act of 1872 had opened formal education to all children in Scotland, but did not provide free boots.

Grandpa left school at the age of 12 and was in charge of the fifth pair of horses on a farm owned by two spinster ladies. As he was only five foot four inches tall as an adult, these Clydesdale horses must have seemed enormous to him. Another farmer, George Bennett, later wrote a glowing testimonial for the now 16-year-old David.

Eventually, David went to Aberdeen, following in the footsteps of his eldest brother, William, to train as a marine engineer at Alexander Hall & Co. Probably at least one other brother also did this. The manager of the Engineering Workshop was Alexander Gray (to be my maternal great-grandfather). Grandpa lodged with a family called Imlach.

Photographs of this time show Grandpa looking very dapper, sporting a wonderful moustache and holding a cane. He must have caught the eye of the

A pair of photographs of Maggie and David taken not long before their wedding on 22 August 1902.

manager's daughter, Margaret, or Maggie, for on 22 August 1902, they were married at the Bon Accord Hotel in Aberdeen. The bride wore a beige and lilac dress with a white veil and held a wonderful feathered fan. Granny kept this in a box and we were allowed to touch it under supervision. Granny, who had had to leave school at the age of 11 to help her

Postcard sent to David's daughter Margaret from Hamburg during one of the Rubislaw's voyages.

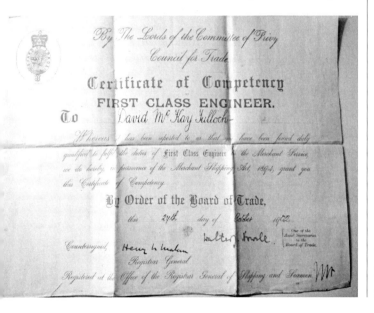

mother look after her brothers, used to say that she could have passed her Chief Engineer's certificate, as she helped Grandpa with his studies.

Grandpa must have gained his engineer's certificate as quite a young man. In 1901, he was staying with his brother William and his family in Govan. He obtained his 1st Class Engineer's Certificate in 1902.

He sailed with the China Mutual Company (which became the Blue Funnel Line) and was on the Glen Gelder before joining the *Rubislaw* as Chief Engineer. These shorter voyages to Hamburg were more suitable for a seaman with young children.

There are postcards sent from Hamburg to his daughter, Margaret, telling her that the voyage went well and when they expected to return to Aberdeen. It is amazing that the postcard would reach home before he did. That would not, I think, be possible today.

Granny and Grandpa had four children: Margaret Jane Anne Tulloch, born 24 June 1903; David Alexander Tulloch, born 26 November 1904; Eveline (Eva) Milton Smith Tulloch, born 14 October 1908; Douglas McKay Tulloch, born 23 November 1911.

Tragically, David died, aged three years one month, from meningitis. Aunt Margaret told me how he kept saying, "I have sic a sair headie". I think Grandpa was at sea when it happened. Carefully preserved are the black-edged receipts for the purchase of the lair and the funeral costs.

I remember going with Grandpa on the bus to tend David's grave at Allenvale Cemetery, where he had planted a pretty little rose. Several years ago, I saw roses of the same variety at Kellie Castle in Fife. Reading the label, I discovered that this rose was

Eva, Douglas and Margaret c1912

called Little White Pet and that it was introduced in the early 1900s. David was sorely missed and often talked of. As a young child, I realised how upset Grandpa was when we visited the grave.

In late July 1914, Grandpa set sail on the *S.S. Rubislaw* for Hamburg. When they reached the River Elbe, no pilot ship appeared to escort them, but the captain sailed on and unloaded. Later, mines were laid and ships were lost trying to negotiate the Elbe. When Britain declared war on Germany, it looked at first as if the *Rubislaw* would be permitted to return to Aberdeen. Cargo was loaded and passengers were accommodated but, after delays, the authorities forbade them to sail, so the cargo had to be unloaded and the passengers turned away. The ship had to anchor out in the Elbe and only the captain was allowed ashore to collect supplies from time to time.

Later, the ship was impounded and the seamen taken off and put on rotting hulks on the Elbe. Conditions were terrible. Finally, in early November, the men were interned at Ruhleben, a racecourse near Spandau outside Berlin.

The men were housed in the filthy, brick-built stables, now called barracks, with little or no heating. Conditions were grim and the diet awful. Grandpa kept an intermittent diary in a tiny black notebook throughout his four-year internment. Most of the entries describe the food, which he found almost uneatable. He was very cold, very hungry and had to sleep on straw on the stone floor of Barrack 9, Box 19.

Eventually, parcels started to arrive and you can tell from his diary entries how much these mean to him. "Parcel, received eatables from home, thank God". At the start, my grandmother had to send food. Delivery was by the Red Cross, via Switzerland, so bread was mouldy by the time it arrived and goodness knows what state the butter was in.

Grandpa's feet were very painful, so my grandmother sent out a new pair of boots, but they never reached him. Her new strategy was to send one boot, then the other, weeks later. This must have made a huge impression on my Uncle Douglas, then a four-year-old boy. When Grandpa was released in 1918, Douglas (now seven years old) and the family were waiting at Aberdeen Station to greet this father he barely remembered. Suddenly Douglas cried out, "There's my Daddy. It's him, he's wearing the boots!".

Some of the Aberdonians in the camp wanted to

send greetings to the people of Aberdeen on their first Christmas of internment, to let the families know that they were safe. To choose who would send the greeting on behalf of the 16 men, names were pulled out of a hat and Grandpa's name was drawn. It is therefore his signature which appears at the end of the letter and he receives season's greetings in rhyme from the Lord Provost of Aberdeen. The article was published in the newspaper and the families were reassured that their loved ones were safe.

I don't remember Grandpa speaking about daily camp life very much. He would have been one of the older men in the camp. He must have missed Captain Walker, his fellow officer, when he was released due to ill health. Mrs Walker used to visit Granny and the family in Aberdeen. Grandpa may have played a bit of football as he could still kick a football in his eighties on family picnics. He learned leather work and he used to speak some German to us and sing the camp song and recited the Ruhleben Alphabet [*see overleaf*].

66, Osborne Pl.

Dear Daddy,
I hope you are well. I have a cold, but I am some better. I am sorry your feet are sore, and I hope they will soon be better. I am a bit bigger since you went away, but I believe you would know me fine.
With love and kisses,
From Eva.

The Ruhleben A.B.C.

A. is for all of us locked up here
B for the Blighters who want give us beer
C. for the Canteen you never get near
D. for the dust heaps - they dont smell - no fear
F for the football they wont let you play
G for "Gott mit us" at last so they say
H for the hope that will get out some day
I for the Ikeys who are Englishmen true
J for the jails that the British go to
K stands for William & all of his set
L for the licking we hope they will get
M for the march and it is a d-d bore
N for the news we dont get of the war
O for the odours that come from the bogs
P for the pork in the soup fit for hogs
Q for the queues in the muck & the cold

R for the rumours a hundred times told
S for the skilly cooked again & again
T for the trucks we wait for in vain
U stands for eunuchs we might as well be
V the vexation on tasting the tea
W the wash in the morning so cold
X is for Xmas well spent we are told
Y is an Englishman kept like a dog?
Z is the shape you assume on the bog.

This is the end of the Ruhleben song
We'll sing it in England before very long
So merry, so merry, so merry are we
And Ruhleben camp is the one place for me
Your soup & your skilly, your coffee and bread
And a nice German coffin as soon as you're dead.

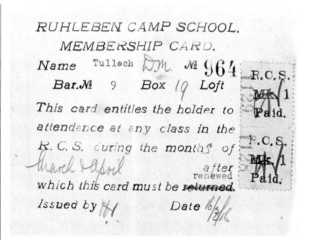

Name Tulloch DM. № 964

Bar. № 9 Box 19 Loft

This card entitles the holder to attendance at any class in the R.C.S. during the months of March & April after renewed which this card must be returned.

Issued by H Date 16/3/16

R.C.S.
Mk 1
Paid.

R.C.S.
Mk 1
Paid.

In recent years, we have been able to piece together information about his gardening. He became a member of the Ruhleben Horticultural Society and of the Camp School. I have his membership cards for both. His name also appears on the list of prisoners who manually dug out a three-foot layer of sand from half the internal oval of the racecourse. This was no mean feat and was rewarded with a small sum of money which he could send home.

In his letters to my grandmother he writes about "the caterpillar" eating their crops and hopes for more sun to ripen their tomatoes. Ruhleben was where he acquired all his knowledge of gardening and for the rest of his life he owned large gardens which he kept immaculately and in which he grew a huge variety of vegetables, fruit and flowers.

As a young child following him round his garden and helping him to plant potatoes, peas, nasturtiums, dahlias, etc., I just accepted his amazing knowledge of gardening. I now realise how he had gained all this expertise.

I learned from the RHS that one of the firms which supplied Ruhleben with seeds and tubers was Smiths of Aberdeen. I still remember accompanying Grandpa on the bus into the city centre to that very same firm to buy his seed potatoes and seeds for the coming spring. The RHS had put out a request for seeds and tubers to be donated and Smiths was one of the firms which volunteered to do so. I have discovered that George Wyllie was the son of the owner of Smiths and he was a fellow internee. Smiths donated sweet pea seeds to Ruhleben where 83 varieties of sweet peas were grown.

Grandpa's upbringing in the harsh winters of the Scottish Highlands and his occupation on ships where he lived and worked in similar cramped conditions, with long separations from his family, stood him in good stead for coping with the rigours of the internment camp.

His faith may have helped him throughout his long separation. I have the Bible given to him by his parents on his 21st birthday. He attended church whenever he could, even as a very old man.

Back home in Aberdeen, the start of the war must have left sailors' families extremely worried. It seemed as if the *Rubislaw* had just disappeared. Maggie, my grandmother, was left with three children aged 11, six and three, and very little income, but she was nothing if not resourceful. She divided the house in two and let one half to gain some income. Records show that the house was "heavily bonded". She took in washing and grew some vegetables.

Granny had trained as a milliner when young and was an expert dressmaker. Even in her 80s, I remember her laying cloth on the floor and just cutting out a garment without a pattern. She used a leather belt and pad when knitting socks, and she also crocheted. My mother said that friends gave Granny their cast-off clothes which she would take apart and sew new clothes for the children. In photographs, the three are well dressed. She would rip out old woolen garments and reknit jumpers and socks for the children. She had relatives who were shoemakers and she obtained a last and tools so that she could repair the children's boots and shoes. She would work hard away into the wee small hours and these late nights became a lifelong habit.

Then she tried taking in lodgers. One of them was an Englishman, a naval officer who had been posted to Aberdeen. I think he was a nice enough man, but they thought he was a bit la-di-dah. When Granny asked if there was anything he would like, he asked if it was possible to have some spinach. It was not something they had ever eaten, but Granny went and bought some and was amazed what a huge bag of leaves she got. Thinking he couldn't possibly eat all that, she put a handful of leaves in the water, only to discover that when it was boiled it had shrunk down to almost nothing at all.

The family was surviving on nineteen shillings and sixpence (almost a pound) a week. One of Grandpa's letters from the camp urges her to contact the *Rubislaw*'s owners to ascertain whether she is being paid the correct sum by the Board of Trade's rules. He might also have sent her some money from the camp if he could from his 'earnings'.

Her income was increased eventually due to a rather strange occurrence. One day, two smartly dressed Englishmen rang the doorbell. They enquired if they were speaking to Margaret Tulloch, wife of David Tulloch at present in prison camp in Germany. Maggie was understandably concerned as to whether anything had happened to Grandpa. They reassured her and produced some of her letters to Ruhleben and asked if she had written these. "Yes," she replied, then asked angrily why her husband had not received these letters. They asked her to produce an example of her handwriting. "I dinnae hae time tae write apart frae these!" she said. Eventually, she found her shopping list and handed it over. "Ah," one gentleman said to the other, "she does it all the time."

Scattered all over the paper were little dots of ink. Granny, who, it must be remembered, had left school at age 11, would pause to think as she wrote and rest her pen on the paper, leaving ink dots. Her recent letters to Grandpa had been under scrutiny in London for several weeks as there had been a suspicion that these dots represented a code. The gentlemen were reassured and apologised. They asked if she was managing financially and, when she described their situation, they said that they would try to help. The authorities later agreed to supplement her income by an extra pound a week.

When daughter Margaret became 14, she had to leave school and find work to help the family finances. This was hard, as Margaret was clever and would have loved to stay at school. She got a job in a local lawyer's office, collecting rents, earning, I think, five shillings a week. Granny didn't think that was enough, and sent her back to tell the solicitor that her mother said she was worth more than that to her just helping around the house. Margaret was very nervous, but the man roared with laughter and agreed to pay her seven shillings and sixpence.

The job was no easy task for a young girl, as many tenants refused to pay. Apparently, Granny told her daughter to go back and tell these people that her father was a prisoner in Germany and that if they didn't pay their rent, she would lose her job and her family would suffer. This tactic worked.

There is a glowing reference written by the lawyer for Margaret when she left the firm 10 years later to move to Fife with her family. Eva, who was 10 when her father returned home, was lucky and able to stay at school and take Highers before attending teacher Training College.

My mother said the wait on the day of Grandpa's homecoming had been terrible. "We were so excited and the train was delayed because of the dreadful accident." There had not been enough room on the train bringing the liberated internees

Photo of Granny, Eva, Grandpa, Douglas and Margaret not long after the war and his homecoming, standing together in countryside.

home. A few men had climbed on to the roof and were killed as the train went through a tunnel. I have researched rail accidents in Scotland for December 1918, but can find no record of such a tragedy. However there was such a tragic accident at this time in Belgium. My mother, who lived to be over 99, retained a very good memory until the day she died, so there must be a basis for her recollection.

The records show that Grandpa returned home in December, 1918. In 1919, he was back at sea and on the *Rubislaw*, by now returned from Germany, but not sailing from Aberdeen. According to

ID and service certificate. This is dated 4th February 1919. I think the photograph shows how he has aged after over four years internment.

Eva with Morag the dog, Grandpa and Margaret.

his diary, he has travelled to South Shields, with a careful record kept of expenses – train travel, meals and accommodation. There is an account in one of his notebooks of a voyage to Valencia.

The *Rubislaw*, in a sorry state, did not return to Aberdeen until 1921, an event recorded in the local press. There was a protracted lawsuit in an attempt to recoup costs for the ship owners from the German government.

In 1924, Grandpa, now aged almost 50, stopped going to sea and the family moved to Anstruther in Fife. From 1925, they lived in a substantial Victorian villa with a large garden. In the background of family photographs can be seen vegetable crops, fruit, flowers, cold frames, etc. He attended gardening lectures locally and in a little notebook he kept notes of useful gardening tips. Grandpa was now employed by U.S.H.D. Insurance Company of Peterhead, travelling to ports in Scotland and England to survey boilers on fishing vessels. Margaret worked in the office of a clothing factory and Eva and Douglas went to Waid Academy. I do have

Grandpa's 1953 gardening notebook showing notes taken at a meeting in the local school in Anstruther.

My mother, Eva, and her brother, Douglas, in the Anstruther garden with cold frame and planted borders behind.

vague memories of Grandpa's 'office' with green lino flooring and an old-fashioned telephone – the home-working of the time.

Grandpa retired when he was 73 and he and Granny moved back to Aberdeen in 1949-50 to a semi-detached house. Not many men of his age would have contemplated moving to a house with such a large garden to maintain. I used to 'help' him in the holidays. He showed endless patience and never seemed irritated by any questions or requests. His potatoes were large, his peas deliciously sweet and his strawberries perfect. As I helped him to pick his strawberry crop, he would say, "Keep whistling, Doreen!" (You can't whistle and munch fruit at the same time.)

Towards the end of his life, I helped him to cut the grass and edges, but he continued to grow his vegetables, fruit and flowers until his death in 1968. He had lived through two world wars and seen society change completely. He had seen the invention of the motor car and aeroplane and watched men go into space. To many, he was just an ordinary old man but, as with many others of his generation, his life had been by no means ordinary.

Doreen on Grandpa's knee in the Aberdeen garden with a tray of his strawberries.

Select bibliography

Bury, Herbert. MY VISIT TO RUHLEBEN. University of Toronto Press, 1917

Cohen, Israel. THE RUHLEBEN PRISON CAMP: A RECORD OF NINETEEN MONTHS INTERNMENT. Methuen & Co, 1917

Dowling, Timothy C. PERSONAL PERSPECTIVES: WORLD WAR I. ABC-CLIO, 2006. (Chapter on Prisoners of War in World War I: British and allied civilian internees at Ruhleben Camp, Germany.)

Foreman, Lewis. IN RUHLEBEN CAMP, in *First World War Studies* 2/1, 2011, pp.27-40

Gerard, James W. MY FOUR YEARS IN GERMANY. George H. Doran Company, 1917

Ketchum, John Davidson. RUHLEBEN: A PRISON CAMP SOCIETY. University of Toronto Press, 1965

Molony, William. PRISONERS AND CAPTIVES. Macmillan & Co, 1933

Powell, J. THE HISTORY OF RUHLEBEN: A RECORD OF BRITISH ORGANISATION IN A PRISON CAMP IN GERMANY. Collins, 1919

Sladen, Douglas. IN RUHLEBEN: LETTERS FROM A PRISONER TO HIS MOTHER. Hurst and Blackett, 1917

Stibbe, Matthew. BRITISH CIVILIAN INTERNEES IN GERMANY: THE RUHLEBEN CAMP 1914-18. Manchester University Press, 2008.

Strub-Ronayne, Elgin. CABBAGE SOUP AGAIN: THE HARDSHIPS AND RESILIENCE OF MEN HELD IN GERMANY'S RUHLEBEN PRISON CAMP, in *Centenary News, 10 February 1914*. Published in centenarynews.com

Other sources

The Ruhleben Archive at the RHS Lindley Library

The British Newspaper Archive